W9-BMU-603

What Winners
Do to Win!

To be the winner
you know you
are!

Nicki Joy

What Winners Do to Win!

The 7 Minutes a Day That Can Change Your Life

Nicki Joy

WILEY

JOHN WILEY & SONS, INC.

Copyright © 2003 by Nicki Joy & Associates, Inc. All rights reserved.

Published by John Wiley & Sons, Inc., Hoboken, New Jersey.
Published simultaneously in Canada.

No part of this publication may be reproduced, stored in a retrieval system, or transmitted in any form or by any means, electronic, mechanical, photocopying, recording, scanning, or otherwise, except as permitted under Section 107 or 108 of the 1976 United States Copyright Act, without either the prior written permission of the Publisher, or authorization through payment of the appropriate per-copy fee to the Copyright Clearance Center, Inc., 222 Rosewood Drive, Danvers, MA 01923, (978) 750-8400, fax (978) 750-4470, or on the web at www.copyright.com. Requests to the Publisher for permission should be addressed to the Permissions Department, John Wiley & Sons, Inc., 111 River Street, Hoboken, NJ 07030, (201) 748-6011, fax (201) 748-6008, e-mail: permcoordinator@wiley.com.

Limit of Liability/Disclaimer of Warranty: While the publisher and author have used their best efforts in preparing this book, they make no representations or warranties with respect to the accuracy or completeness of the contents of this book and specifically disclaim any implied warranties of merchantability or fitness for a particular purpose. No warranty may be created or extended by sales representatives or written sales materials. The advice and strategies contained herein may not be suitable for your situation. The publisher is not engaged in rendering professional services, and you should consult a professional where appropriate. Neither the publisher nor author shall be liable for any loss of profit or any other commercial damages, including but not limited to special, incidental, consequential, or other damages.

For general information on our other products and services please contact our Customer Care Department within the United States at 800-762-2974, outside the United States at (317) 572-3993 or fax (317) 572-4002.

Wiley also publishes its books in a variety of electronic formats. Some content that appears in print may not be available in electronic books. For more information about Wiley products, visit our web site at www.wiley.com.

Library of Congress Cataloging-in-Publication Data:

Joy, Nicki.
    What winners do to win! : the 7 minutes a day that can change your life / Nicki Joy.
        p. cm.
    ISBN 0-471-26577-2 (cloth : alk. paper)
    1. Success. 2. Self-realization. I. Title: 7 minutes a day that can change your life. II. Title
        BF637.S8 J69 2003
        158—dc21   2002152718

Printed in the United States of America.
10 9 8 7 6 5 4 3 2 1

*This book is dedicated to the one person
who most inspired me to win:
Harry Louis Berke,
my departed and dearly loved father.*

Contents

Acknowledgments

I want to express my utmost thanks and appreciation to Matt Holt, Senior Editor at John Wiley & Sons. His encouragement, insight, assistance, skill, and attitude helped me beyond words in making this book happen. I also want to thank my dear friend, Susan Kane-Benson, for all her support and belief in me. I am blessed to have her in my life. To my husband, Steve, and two great sons, Bill and Mitch: I appreciate all their faith in me and the gift of love they have given me. And to my assistant, Chris Einhorn: I extend my gratitude for her input, my thankfulness for her dedication, and my appreciation for her work and loyalty.

Introduction

In talking to tens of thousands of people each year, I am repeatedly reminded that winning means different things to different people. For some, winning conjures up the image of competing with others and coming in first place. For others, it means obtaining that promotion or getting that raise. For still others, winning may mean enjoying the lifestyle of the rich and famous or perhaps being able to drop out and live a simple, unencumbered life on a remote island.

Putting personal definitions aside, as we live our lives, we all want to feel like a winner. However, it's been said that in this game called life, no one can really win; all we can do is play it. Well to me, winning *is* playing it—playing it in such a way that your life is comfortable, happy, enjoyable, positive, rewarding, and fun. That's my definition of winning, and if those elements of life appeal to you, this book will help you get in that winner's circle. If you're already in that circle, this book will help you stay there.

When playing life to win, you must first know the rules of the game. This book has the rules; and those rules were developed by studying winners for over 30 years. Those rules came about by uncovering the universal qualities that winners have and by examining the principles they live by. Though you may know some of these rules already, many of them discussed in this book are guaranteed to surprise you. For example, did you know that expecting a lot, wanting it now, doing the obvious, and welcoming change are all qualities that winners posses?

Interestingly enough, however, it doesn't matter what one's personal definition of winning is; if that definition is positive, realistic, equitable, and legal, most winners actually follow the same rules to win.

After knowing those rules, the next step in winning involves developing the right strategy. That means embracing the right mindset. It entails figuring out how to use the rules to your advantage. Doing that doesn't involve finding loopholes, cutting corners, bending those rules, or outrunning and outwitting the others playing the game. Instead, the winning strategy involves positioning yourself to win by focusing on elevating yourself, rather than beating out the competition.

Nineteenth-century satirical columnist George Ade made us doubt our winning chances when he said, "Anyone can win…unless there happens to be a second entry." Though competition of course is part of life and does ensure survival of the fittest, in my definition of winning the number of entrees has nothing to do with your chances to succeed. In fact, in my definition of winning, adopting the strategy and mindset to compete with yourself first and foremost is essential. Yes, wanting to be better is the first winning mindset. This book will help you easily develop that mindset and strategy and launch you off on to greater personal and professional heights.

Of course, beside knowing the rules and having a mindset to win you still have to get out there and play the game. Playing takes action; and it is that *play* that hangs people up. In terms of taking action, people fall into three categories: (1) those who cannot be moved, (2) those who can be moved, and (3) those who do indeed move. This book will help you make the right moves. It will help you move in the right direction by giving you simple steps to take every day that will place you in that winning life position. These steps will enable you to quickly prepare yourself every day for a jump-start on the next one. These steps will help you get others to want to work harder for you. These steps will help you better motivate and condition yourself for success.

Changing your life begins with changing your mind, and all you need is 7 minutes a day to get started—just 7 minutes a day—to read one chapter and then follow through with the exercises or steps suggested. The rules, mindsets, and action-plans presented in this book, if adhered to, are guaranteed to change your life course and make you a winner. Though most people don't know how to win, this book teaches one big, wonderful, heartening truth—anyone can!

What Winners
Do to Win!

Winning Principle

Winners Have a Sense of Maturity

It has been said that you can only be young once, but you can be immature indefinitely. Since I love to laugh and have fun and since I do everything in my power to blend business with pleasure, I have, in my life, run across others who have called me immature. Quite frankly, that label has really bothered me, so much in fact that I recently spoke to my pediatrician about it. Fortunately, he told me that I'm just fine and advised that I should just keep on doing what I'm doing—and I intend to!

Winners know that maturity has nothing to do with age, education, or even experiences in life. Winners know that maturity has nothing to do with being staid, stodgy, or stuffy. Winners know that maturity is not contingent on being conservative, serious, or conventional. Though a child can seem mature for his age, winners also know that maturity is usually not associated with youth. That's because the elements of maturity involve reason; and the ability to reason takes time to develop. As the German proverb says, "Reason does not come before years."

Many feel that youth, because it's the most carefree time of life, must also be the happiest time. For most of us, however, that will not prove true at all. The happiest times in our lives are times when we are thinking the most motivating, intelligent, and productive thoughts. Therefore, as we grow in years, we really get happier, as long as we can understand how to live a productive, motivating life with a degree of reason and intelligence behind it.

William Lyon Phelps, noted writer and Yale English professor, said, "To say that youth is happier than maturity is like saying that the view from the bottom of the tower is better than the view from the top. As we ascend, the range of our view widens immensely; the horizon is pushed farther away. Finally as we reach the summit it seems as if the world is at our feet."

Though in reality, you don't have to reach the summit to be considered mature, you do indeed have to have basic reasoning power. To have basic reasoning power, you need to be rational. Some people never develop a sense of rationality even as they advance on in years.

Albert Ellis developed a type of treatment called Rational Emotive Therapy, which has been proven to work for many of his patients. Ellis believed that people have problems because they are illogical or irrational to begin with. Based on that theory, he developed a Rational Behavior Inventory to see where his patients stood in terms of their degree of rationality. Ellis has formulated a list of irrational ideas that he believes are strongly associated with mental distress. I believe that some of them have a bottom-line bearing on one's ability to reason in general, which can therefore negatively or positively affect one's ability to be mature. So, to see if your maturity is in jeopardy because your irrational ideas are hampering your sense of reason, see how you would answer the following questions devised by Ellis.

1. You *must* have the love and approval of everyone important in your life. ___Yes ___No

2. You must be thoroughly competent, adequate, and achieving in everything you do. ___Yes ___No

3. People who mistreat you are bad, wicked, or villainous and deserve to be severely punished. ___Yes ___No

4. It is impossible to control your feelings when bad things happen. ___Yes ___No

5. When a situation becomes dangerous or frightening, you have no choice but to become preoccupied and upset about it. ___Yes ___No

6. It is easier to avoid life's difficulties rather than to face them head on. ___Yes ___No

7. Your life is determined by your past, and it is impossible to do anything to ever change this. ___Yes ___No

8. All problems have good solutions. ___Yes ___No

Chances are, if you agree with any of the preceding statements, you harbor some irrational thoughts that can indeed affect your reasoning power. Since weak reasoning power affects maturity, those wanting to win should examine this issue.

When you reach a stage of maturity you have ripened, blossomed, and have attained a peak developmental level. The good news is that when your maturity level goes up, it doesn't ever have to come down.

In being able to determine one's level of maturity, I have noticed that nine abilities come into play. These nine abilities appear to strongly help people seize opportunity, project a winning persona, position themselves for even greater success, cope with life's frustration, and fortify their staying power. These nine abilities are:

1. **The ability to do a job without supervision.**

2. **The ability to complete, without prodding, the job that you started.**

3. **The ability to carry money in your pocket without having to spend it on something.**

4. **The ability to carry an injustice without feeling the need for revenge.**

5. **The ability to anticipate—to see down the road.**

6. **The ability to be discreet, to have self-censorship and tact.**

7. **The ability to think about the repercussions and consequences of your actions or inactions.**

8. **The ability to take blame when warranted.**

9. **The ability to learn from experience.**

1. The Ability to Do a Job without Supervision

It's amazing how many people cannot discipline themselves to work on something unless someone is looking over their shoulder. So many people actually need the threat of reprimand to do the work they have to do. They have little momentum of their own, lack a sense of continuum, can't cope with frustration on any level, and pride of work doesn't really enter into the picture. After all, it's just a job, they feel.

Though winners, like others, may become overwhelmed with a project—and may need the help of colleagues—they all have a sense of pride in their own ability to handle as much of the given task as possible on their own. Yes, winners know how to work through annoyances. If doable, they will try their best to work it out themselves.

Winners supervise themselves, so to speak. Though they can feel thwarted while tackling a job, they know how to override it and move on. They have the knack of coming up with new strategies, new thinking, and new game plans to plow forward. Winners know that frustration is a part of life. From a business perspective, coping with it is an important element in being able to forge ahead. From a more personal standpoint, coping with frustration is part of keeping any good relationship going.

Frustration is one of the chief contributing factors that deters people from doing what they have to do. Winners, quite frankly, have a higher frustration tolerance than others, and rely on themselves to overcome potential setbacks more quickly.

2. The Ability to Complete the Job That You Started without Prodding

Winners are not only self-starters, but also self-finishers. Though winners may lose interest in a project, instead of dropping it or procrastinating, they tend to do what it takes to get over it fast, so they can get on to something better. Winners accept the consequences of commitment. They are true to their word. They say they'll get it done, and they do get it done. They know how to divide those more complex tasks down into manageable parts. They know how to complete one section at a time, and they also feel free to reward themselves along the way for accomplishing parts of the job.

The commitment toward completion is really part of the winner's creed. Where others may only get involved in the task, winners are committed to it. It's like ham and eggs. The chicken was involved but the pig was committed. Certainly, winners do not have to die for their cause, but they put forth all the effort needed to make it happen.

3. The Ability to Carry Money in Your Pocket without Spending It

Confidentially, this remains one of the aspects of maturity that I am still working on. When thinking about spending, I remember what Jackie Mason said: " I don't have to worry about money; I have enough money to last me the rest of my life…as long as I don't buy anything."

Yes, money does indeed burn a hole in some of our pockets. This often happens to people who never had money in the past and have it now. The ability to spend and buy becomes somewhat of an aphrodisiac. Managing money is an art as well as a science, and mastering that art and science takes practice.

There is a reason why a large percentage of lottery winners turn out to be stone broke within 18 to 24 months after winning those big bucks. They lack money-management experience. Yes, how many times do we hear of new millionaires who become bankrupt for no conceivable reason except for the fact that they could not control their everyday spending? Finding the balance between enjoying one's money and frittering it away is often difficult, but it's indeed a sign of maturity.

4. The Ability to Carry an Injustice without Feeling the Need for Revenge

It's been said that a grudge is a very heavy burden to bear. Though psychologists say that revenge is a basic human impulse and can in some cases not only discourage power abuse by authorities but can restore a person's damaged status, winners know that generally speaking revenge can not only be harmful to the victim but hurtful to the avenger. Winners may not forget the injustice, but they usually do have the ability to forgive it. Forgiveness is an essential part of moving forward and in a sense, a prerequisite to freedom. Grudges take up a great deal of energy. They tie up your thoughts and slow down your actions. Though many feel that it's far easier to forgive others once you have gotten back at them, it's hard to be a winner if your life is ruled by ongoing bitterness and retaliation. Winners know that their energy needs to be positive. Their energy must be spent on the present and the future, not on the past.

5. The Ability to Anticipate

In business, anticipation is the most strategic sales and marketing weapon there is. Anticipation is the ability to prevent or expedite by taking some advanced action or by doing some future-directed thinking. Winners know that you don't have to be a visionary to take the time to anticipate. Winners stop and think, "How can this play out? How do I need to be prepared for the most likely eventuality?"

It's been said that most people take more time to anticipate their two-week vacation than to anticipate the other 50 weeks of the year. I run into folks all the time who plan their vacations in detail, who get the appropriate maps, sunscreen, beach chairs and margarita mix, but who just let the rest of the year kind of take care of itself. Winners know that there's a window between stimulus and response, and they use that window to prepare, to plan, and to anticipate how to respond. This doesn't mean that they lose the ability to be spontaneous or wing it; it just means that when they're able to benefit from thinking ahead, they meticulously use that tool.

A comedienne once said that no one actually goes to Denny's; they just kind of wind up there. They wind up there because they failed to anticipate the fact that at around noon every day, they get hungry. Perhaps the first place they go to has classed up and is now only accepting reservations; perhaps the second place they check out has now closed down; and perhaps the third restaurant has a huge line. Exasperated, they think, "Hell, let's just go to Denny's." I am sure the marketing folks at Denny's are fine with this. If they know their job, they must be aware of the fact that they basically serve the totally exhausted, the extremely wasted, or those who failed to anticipate.

Recently, I attended a meeting in Manhattan. The client suggested that at 1:00 we should break for lunch. Unfortunately, no plans were made. We wasted over an hour and a half going from one place to the next before we were able to get a table at a decent restaurant. That hour and a half was extremely costly all around.

6. The Ability to Be Discreet, Have Self-Censorship, and Tact

It's hard to teach discretion, but discretion is indeed a sign of maturity. Discretion, as used here, stems from an astuteness, a savvy, an awareness, and a sensitivity to others. Though some claim that being frank, even at the risk of embarrassing others in public, is just being candid and honest, winners know that there really is a time and place for nearly everything. Over the years, I have met many people who had all the makings of going to the moon, but who were also significantly waylaid from getting there because of their inability to know what was appropriate and what was not. Though winners do not play games—for game-playing sake—they do understand that their value to any organization or even to any social group goes up if others can feel comfortable in their presence by knowing that they have that important sense of propriety. How many careers have been damaged by those who tell dirty jokes intrepidly, who reveal their political ties inappropriately, and who embarrass others around them insensitively? Winners know what to say and when to say it. This doesn't mean that they don't make waves; it just means that they know when and where to make them.

It's been said that tact is the ability to put up with someone you'd like to put down. I read that Abraham Lincoln was the master of tact. Once, when asked to comment in front of a crowd about a displeasing portrait that had been painted of him, he said something to the tune of, For the sort of person, who likes this sort of thing, this, is the sort of thing, that sort of person really likes.

7. The Ability to Think about the Repercussions and Consequences of Your Actions or Inactions

There's the story about the businessman who, while traveling to Saudi Arabia, strayed from his group and found himself lost for days in the desert. He was ready to faint from dehydration when he saw a tent ahead with a nomad standing out front. Staggering towards the nomad, the businessman stammered, "Water, please." The nomad replied, " Sorry sir, I have no water, however would you like to buy a nice silk tie?" The businessman screaming back yelled, "I'm dying of thirst. I need water, not a stupid silk tie." The nomad, though startled, responded that over the next sand dune there was a restaurant built around an oasis and surely the parched man could get water there. Now, crawling on hands and knees, the businessman found his way over to that next dune and spotted a tuxedo-clad nomad standing in front of a tent that had the words Oasis Restaurant printed on a sign above it. "May I help you sir?" asked the well-dressed nomad. "Water. Do you have water inside?" gasped the businessman. Answered the nomad, "Of course, we do, sir, but we don't serve anyone without a tie."

I have to say that thinking about the consequences or repercussions of your action or inaction can often serve as the motivational impetus to help you do what needs to be done, especially when you don't want to do it. However, understand that that ability is also tied into maturity. Winners are able to see down the road; they have foresight and are able to think in terms of repercussions. That trait not only helps them plan and prepare better; it often gives them the vision needed to see the true impact of their proposed strategies and actions.

8. The Ability to Accept Blame for a Wrong Doing

How often do you hear people taking credit for the good they do, but no blame for the bad? Children are known to say things like, "I got an A in math, but the teacher gave me an F in history." Yes, it's been said that a great amount of maturing takes place between "it dropped" and "I dropped it." Some people simply can't admit when they make mistakes. The problem always stems from someone else's errors. As one of my bourbon-loving uncles used to say, "I've never been drunk, I've just been over-served."

Winners know that if they won't admit when they make a mistake, they start a trend—and soon no one else in their circle will admit mistakes either. Winners know that from time to time everyone can make an honest mistake, but they also know there is no such thing as an honest cover-up. Winners admit mistakes made, and they also give others clear permission to make some as well. Though for most, the threat of castigation for a mistake creates the wish for an escape route, winners know that the best approach is to go public with the wrong that was done. Honesty saves energy and allows attention to be paid to fixing the problem rather than hiding it. Of course, winners are also aware of Goldfinger's words to James Bond: "One mistake is happenstance, two mistakes are coincidence, but three mistakes are enemy firing action."

9. The Ability to Learn from Experience

Albert Einstein said that insanity is doing the same thing over and over again and expecting different results. Winners are very aware that that can happen, and do everything in their power to learn from experience and avoid making the same mistake twice. It has been said that though the tuition is often so high, experience is still the best teacher. I feel that experience is also a hard teacher, because the test comes first and the lesson surfaces afterwards.

Experience, however, is the thing that enables you to recognize a mistake right after you make it. For many people, the lesson never sinks in. The recognition that "I have been here before" never happens. Dear Abby wrote, "If we could sell our experiences for what they cost us we'd all be millionaires." Yes, it's too bad that experience is usually most needed before we ever manage to actually get it.

Winners, however, have a shorter experiential learning curve than others. It simply takes them less time to get the message.

Now take a moment. Stop and think. How do you stand in terms of your maturity level? Looking at these elements of maturity, how would you rate your abilities? Where do you shine? Where will you need to improve so winning can more easily come your way?

Chapter

2

Winning Principle

Winners Motivate Themselves

Winning begins with an appetite for achievement and success. It's empowering for us to read stories about how others have won. Stories about others provide us with hope and lessons about what it takes to win. For example, when reading about John Brunswick who started the world's biggest billiard-equipment operation, we see energy at work. We learn how thinking outside the box (he was a Swiss carriage maker by trade), being flexible, seeing trends, and having a knack for creating synergy contributed to his amazing success.

Reading about Ray Charles, we learn how in 1946 after getting his big break to sing for Lucky Millinder's band, he bombed. Instead of the praises he expected, Millinder told him, "Ain't good enough kid." We learn how after actually crying for several days at this devastating personal disappointment, Ray picked himself up and began to practice intensely, thereby perfecting his unique style. In life we see how, persistence, and self-motivation are important winning ingredients.

Reading about Supreme Court Justice Sandra Day O'Connor, we learn that as a child she lived with a grandmother who was an incessant talker. Realizing that she couldn't even get her homework done without having her grandmother interrupt, she learned early on the art of focusing and concentrating to achieve the results she wanted.

What especially amazes me, however, is that so many people can read story after story about others' successes and about what others endured to get to where they wanted to go, but still fail to realize that it took **self-initiative** and **self-motivation** to get there.

Traveling three to four days a week, I remain in awe of the fact that—no matter where I am geographically, or who I may be talking to personally or professionally—when someone hears that I'm a sales motivator, the response is nearly always, "Boy, oh boy. I sure could use some motivation in my life and I'd love to find someone to give it to me."

I remain incredulous. Has the concept that motivation comes from within never been taught, or if so, has it been ignored? Has the fact that we are all responsible for motivating ourselves remained elusive? Is it so foreign and unknown that, ultimately, to get the most out of life, we all have to be our own back-up band? Do people not understand that we all have to cultivate our own pump-up power?

Motivation comes from inside, it lies in one's guts, and it's an internal mechanism. However, fortunately for me—since I make my living at it—someone from the outside can help to propel others along in their winning quest. Yes, often someone from the outside can say something in a certain way, teach something with a new twist, present something with a new flair or spin, create a certain mood or feeling that actually can serve to inspire others to better motivate themselves.

Nevertheless, it should be remembered that though outside motivators may indeed lead the horse to water, they still can't make 'em drink; they can only make 'em thirsty. And though thirst is a good first step in making anything happen, it's still unfortunately only a first step.

The concept that motivation has to come ultimately from within, when learned, disheartens a lot of people. Let's face it: It's much easier to put someone else in charge of you. Self-responsibility can be a very heavy burden. It's comforting and hopeful to think that perhaps there's someone out there who can make you do what you know you should.

Winners, however, all seem to eventually understand that:

1. Even if it was possible to find someone else who could be in charge of your own personal motivation, that would be disempowering. Not only would that result in relinquishing control of yourself; it would also drain away the inner confidence we all need for a vital sense of self-worth.

2. While waiting for that elusive, special someone to come along to pump you back up, to reignite your flame, to heal your wounded spirit, you'll wind up waiting much longer to be restored than if you grab the bull by the horns, take charge, and start rebuilding yourself…now…immediately.

3. In this game called life that we all play, everyone gets worn down from time to time. Injustices occur, "it" happens. Being able to raise yourself back up, being able to reboot your own spirits, being able to re-inspire yourself, helps you develop an important muscle that even the finest fitness gyms in America don't develop. It's called your *motivational muscle*.

Okay, let us talk about that *motivational muscle*. To develop it, you first need to embrace three critical motivational concepts:

1. *Self-motivation is part of your basic self-maintenance.* To winners, it's as important as brushing their teeth, taking a bath, and eating. Granted, though those aspects of self-maintenance are more connected with grooming or your physical upkeep, being able to motivate yourself is directly correlated with another type of grooming—your mental upkeep. Yes, motivation is part of your psychological self-maintenance and it's serious stuff.

2. *As with all maintenance efforts, engaging in the self-motivational process by building up that motivational muscle is not a one-time process.* Are there any maintenance programs that are? You don't put oil in your car once and say; "Well, I'm done with that." You don't eat once and say, "I'm full forever." You don't brush your teeth once and say, "I'll never touch a toothbrush again." You don't bathe once and say, "Now, I'm clean for the rest of my life!" Well, motivation works the same way. It's something you do for yourself on an ongoing basis as part of your own preservation perpetuation and winning life path. In other words, getting yourself motivated is not a one-time event; it is an ongoing, never-ending program.

3. *Motivation is not for those who are weak; it is for those who are tough.* Motivation is not for the inadequate; it

is for the intelligent. Motivation is not just necessary for beginners; motivation is important to the seasoned professionals as well. Superstars, in fact, need motivation the most because they use up so much of themselves on a day-to-day basis. They put so much of themselves into their work, their projects, their goals. Their passion is evident; they put their hearts and souls into what they do. That level of focus and intensity can be very mentally draining and physically exhausting. Winners know they need to have that motivational muscle in shape as that gives them the energy, drive, will, resilience, and the staying power to keep at it.

4. *Though motivation, as already stated, comes from the inside, developing that motivational muscle starts from the outside.* Yes, as with developing any other muscle in your body, you can't build it up by *thinking* about going to the gym. You (unfortunately) have to show up at the gym and actually work out.

   Working out requires repetitive physical exercises. It requires a physical regimen. Well, winners know that the same is true when it comes to developing that motivational muscle. Yes, believe it or not, a specific type of repetitive behavior will help you start building up your motivational muscle as well.

Let's take a look then at some seemingly inconsequential, but critical and easy, exercises to get you going in the right direction. Adding these to your daily routine will boost your motivation level. Stick with me here; some of these exercises may seem unrelated to the issue, but they will all serve to better position you on that winning path. To winners, these are the the Essential 16:

1. *As you're getting dressed and ready for work in the morning, turn off the TV and fill your environment with music that makes you want to dance.* Pick out the music that moves you. It doesn't matter if it's opera, reggae, country, folk, rock, fusion, new age, hip-hop or salsa—make certain that you can hear it loud and clear as you prepare for your day. One of my business associates had all his television aerials removed. He told me that he felt it was the moral parallel of a prostate operation.

2. *Start collecting motivational sayings, platitudes, or quotes that are meaningful to you.* Plant them around your home in conspicuous places—on the fridge, on the microwave, on your mirror, or on your tie rack. Whenever you see them, reread them for daily affirmations. These messages should serve one purpose and one purpose alone—to make you feel good. I can always rely on the message glued to my bathroom mirror to do just that for me. It says, "Objects in mirror appear larger than they really are." Perfect!

3. *When you walk around, make a conscious effort to move more vigorously, swing your arms, and if you can (without attracting too much attention) hum a tune.*

These little acts will release those endorphins that actually make you feel happier and rejuvenated.

4. *Deliver a genuine compliment to someone everyday.* The act of complimenting has a double-barrel benefit. It makes the compliment-getter as well as the compliment-giver feel good.

5. *Monitor your me-mail.* (No, I don't mean e-mail.) In other words, start immediately to examine what you say when you talk to yourself. We all engage in self-talk; the point is to be aware of it and make sure it has a positive spin. Interestingly enough, most people usually say negative things to themselves: "I'm such a jerk," "I'll never learn," "I can't possibly get this done in time," "I'll never amount to anything."

Winners know that life is a game of ricochets, whereby their beliefs and behaviors—their thoughts and their actions—eventually bounce back to them with amazing precision. Therefore, winners know the incredible significance of the words they speak to themselves, about themselves.

Though action is what counts in life, it all starts with your thoughts. So, monitor those thoughts, as they will dictate your actions. Then watch your actions, because they turn into your habits. Of course you must examine your habits, because they work together to determine your characer, and your chacter—without question—eventually determines your fate.

So, what are some of those statements that you should include in your self-talk? Well, here are just a few ideas of what you can say to yourself that will start the ball rolling in a positive, productive way and start building up that motivational muscle.

"I'm great at what I do."

"I know this business inside and out."

"I believe in the benefit of what I am selling and can help others see those benefits too."

"I can make this happen."

"I'm one of the best there is in this field."

"I'm a valuable person to this company."

"I'm hardworking, loyal, and honest. Those are fantastic qualities."

Remember, the most influential person in your life is you! You must, therefore, be very aware of what you say to yourself. As writer Louise Hay says, "Be gentle with yourself, be kind to yourself. Treat yourself as someone you really loved."

6. *Always be in the process of learning something new.* It doesn't matter if it's elementary Italian, Indian cooking, or a Power Point course—have a place to go that helps you grow at least once a week. And, do not miss a class.

7. *Force yourself to smile as broadly as you can even before you open your eyes in the morning.* Then, as you take your first look into a mirror (and this can be tantamount to torture), smile broadly again and hold that pose for 10 seconds.

8. *Start getting into the habit of dealing with the most stressful things as early as possible each day.* In other words, get it over with so you can feel a sense of accomplishment and move on. Remember that old saying, "If you have to swallow a bull frog, you don't want to look at it too long."

9. *Work to avoid gossiping, bad-mouthing, blaming, or complaining.* Now, I know that by doing this, some of you may not have much to say for a while—and your communication style may be temporarily hampered. But you will soon see how better things look and go when you avoid scandalous and idle chatter.

10. *Force yourself to be enthusiastic.* Henry Ford said, "You can do anything if you have enthusiasm." I don't know if this strategy worked when Ford had to deal with the Firestone Tire folks, but the message still holds a great deal of truth.

11. *Since "good moods" spur self-motivation, recognize when you're in a bad mood and then make a conscious effort to turn it around.* Winners know that they can, at the very least, avoid continuing a bad-mood cycle.

Few people are happy all the time (except those perhaps who spend a few weekends each year out on an institutional pass). Though winners understand that bad moods happen, they treat them differently than most people do.

When most people are in a bad mood, they actually tend to perpetuate that cycle; they tend to keep the downer going. They may do this by withdrawing from others, crawling into bed, burying themselves in a disturbing or sleazy book, rereading an annoying letter, reconnecting with a troubled person, or gluing themselves to the couch to watch the dysfunctional, depraved, and demented on Jerry Springer or Riki Lake. All the preceding activities actually serve to do something harmful: They keep you in that funk.

Winners, when in a bad mood, don't want to stay there. They want to shed the funk. They're not content to let that bad mood dissipate in its own good time. They effect the turn-around process themselves. Yes, even if they're not quite ready to get out there and start punching again—and even if they need to play couch potato a bit longer before tackling that challenge—instead of watching schlock TV, they flip on a comedy. Instead of reading something to keep that mood meter down, they find something encouraging, uplifting, or funny to read. Instead of connecting with a person whose life has gone to hell in a basket, they connect with someone who is supportive, positive, and successful.

A study by Dr. Richard Petty of Ohio State University revealed that the degree of self-esteem that one has is actually tied into how they strive to improve their bad-mood times. People with low self-esteem tend to perpetuate negativity; they seem to flounder in a feeling of hopelessness or helplessness rather than try to change it. People with higher self-esteem, however, tend to work very hard to retrieve their positive life status. Petty said that people who value themselves think that they don't deserve to feel badly. So they exert positive energy into chasing that debilitating gloom away.

In essence, it is important to understand that though when in a bad mood you may not be able to pull yourself totally and immediately out of it, you can at least take some steps to make yourself happier. Winners do!

12. *Exercise the process of consequentiality.* At times, you will notice that focusing in on the good, the potentially positive results, and the benefits of taking action will still not provide you with enough impetus to motivate you sufficiently. When that's the case, tackle self-motivation from the other angle. Start imagining the consequences that inaction will bring you. Start visualizing what might happen if you don't do it.

When I was a kid in school, my father often motivated me to study for a test with this consequence approach. He would say, "I know that studying takes time away from play, and I know it's often boring and hard. However, stop and imagine how you will feel tomorrow, as you sit in that classroom struggling. Think how you will feel when you see the names of those who have passed the test posted on the board and your name is not there. Think about having to take this whole course from beginning to end over again this summer, when other kids are out swimming and biking." Those types of statements frequently worked better than the "you-can-do-it" ones.

Recently, I was out for dinner with a marketing vice president of a public relations firm in Dallas. She said she was having a hard time getting herself psyched up to make the calls she had to make to connect with some of the newer companies in town. We talked about what would happen if she failed to get moving. We talked about her competition getting their foot in the door first. We talked about how she would feel at the next association meeting if she had no new client names to brag about. The next afternoon, she called and told me that hearing the probable consequences of her intended inaction spelled out so specifically was just the kick she needed to get going.

13. *Make a list of the 10 things you most enjoy doing.* Think how long it's been since you've done them? Ignoring your personal happiness for your professional happiness can be demotivating all around.

14. *Examine the negative forces in your life and do everything in your power to eliminate them.* For example, make a conscientious effort to avoid:
    - Dwelling on and perpetuating bad news
    - Hanging around with chronically depressed people
    - Associating with consistently angry coworkers
    - Accepting responsibility without having any authority
    - Cleaning up the poor work of others

15. *Change your "if" language to "when" language.* It's not *if* I get through this project, I'm taking a day off. It's *when* I get through this project, I'm taking a day off.

16. *Check your goals and understand that if one goal area of your life is lagging or faltering, you can concentrate, for now, on getting closer to achieving success in another goal area.*

    Remember if all you're about is your work, you can't be good at your work. So, recheck your goals in all eight areas of your life. Those areas are:
    - Business development
    - Money
    - Mental development
    - Physical fitness (which encompasses health and energy)
    - Social
    - Family

- Spiritual
- Fun

Winners have goals in these eight areas of their lives. Do you?

Ask yourself these questions:

- Are my goals very clear or fuzzy?

- Are they too long range or are they broken down into short-term goals so that I can reward myself enough along the way?

- Are my goals specific enough?

- Are they written down? Do they have to be rewritten?

- Are they dated? Do I have a timetable?

- Are they realistic?

- Am I making myself do one thing every day to get me closer to one of my goals?

It's an extreme waste of time to wait for your ship to come in if you have neglected to send one out to begin with. Sending out your ship begins with setting those personal and professional goals. Understand that nothing is etched in stone. Yes, you can change your goals if you like. However, working on one of your goals everyday in some way is an essential.

Setting goals must become a habit in your life. A study was conducted by Harvard University to determine what happened to those individuals who set goals. Of the 100 students selected, only five actually set goals on a regular, consistent, and methodical basis. Ten years later, Harvard called those 100 people back to participate in a follow-up for this study. They found that the 5 percent who set goals consistently and continued to do so had attained 93 percent of the total net worth of the entire group. Certainly, the amount of wealth that one accumulates is not the only measure of success, happiness, or winning, but it's certainly a common characteristic among many winners.

Get your motivation in gear. Winners know how important that step is. Don't fool yourself—it's all up to you. You can do it. Start now. If not now—when?

Chapter
3

Winning Principle

*Winners Challenge Assumptions,
Take Risks, and Assess
Their Own Abilities*

I am sure that many of you have heard the axiom, "Only 3 percent of the world makes it happen; 7 percent watches it happen; and 90 percent wonders what the hell happened!" Perhaps many of you have also heard the motivational pundits preach that you have to first *believe* you can make it happen in order to actually **make** it happen. Well, let me tell you right now—winners know how valid those statements really are.

For many, "They've gotta see it to believe it." Winners, however, know, "They've gotta believe it to see it." Winners know that in order to see it actually happen, they first have to believe it will indeed happen. Therefore, to set yourself up to win, it is essential for you to examine what you believe.

Belief is a very powerful thing. Do you realize that your beliefs activate your responses? Your beliefs control what you do. Your beliefs determine how you act and how you react. Your beliefs govern the path you take, the choices you make, and how you look at life. Your beliefs control your destiny.

The really frightening thing about our belief systems is that, unfortunately, they do not distinguish between fact and fantasy, between truth and lies, or between reality and imagination.

Consider this scenario. Perhaps a similar incident has happened to you. You just got out of a late-night meeting. You're all alone in a dark and confusing underground garage trying to remember where you parked your car. As you wander around, you think you hear footsteps. You believe you see a tall, looming shadow. You suspect that someone might be following you. Your heart rate escalates from the potential danger you may be facing; you get queasy with fear; you start perspiring; your mind starts racing; your mouth gets dry; your pulse quickens. You finally find your car. You jump in and lock up immediately. You start your engine and exit the underground cavern. Whew, you are safe! You breathe that sigh of relief, and then almost laugh. You realize that you psyched yourself out. The terror you experienced was created by your own imagination. In reality, there was no one out to harm you…you just *believed* that there might have been someone out there.

The amazing thing is that even though nothing happened, even though it was just a suspicion, even though it was just your vivid imagination at work, your body responded the same way it would have responded had the imagined threat been real. You see, it is what you *believed* to be true—not necessarily what actually *was* true—that triggered your behavior.

The example used above depicts a belief-reaction to potential *physical* danger. However, keep in mind that if that potential danger was to be delivered in *mental* form— perhaps in the form of an intimidating, inhibiting, damning, or limiting opinion about your abilities from others—your belief-reactions would have just as much impact on you, and could prove to be even more life damaging. "Oh, there you go again. I'm telling you, you're just as nuts as your Aunt Martha." "Don't go thinking you're smart now; we all know you've got a mind like a sieve." "I haven't selected you for this assignment because I don't feel you can handle it." "You're not going to be good at that, so don't even try." "The marketing department couldn't find a way to make this work. What makes you think you can?" "Our family never had much money, but we did just fine, and so will you with the limited amount of money you can make." "The people we have recruited from your school weren't executive or leadership material, but they did prove to be good followers."

Your beliefs are critical. Your beliefs are the key that unlocks the winning or losing door, no matter what challenges you face. Since your beliefs rule your life, it is almost horrifying to realize that so many beliefs, particularly those about our abilities, have been formulated by others. Yes, from youth through adulthood, we are too often controlled by the beliefs others have handed to us. In fact, even when we finally reach an age when we become smart enough and gutsy enough to doubt the accuracy of what others have told us (or are now telling us) about our abilities, most of us still don't question it. You see, those beliefs that were drilled into us at such an impressionable age, those beliefs that are handed to us now by others, tend not only to remain unchallenged but, amazingly all too often achieve self-acceptance. Yes, we tend to perform as others expected we would.

Fortunately, some people realize sooner or later that perhaps they are more capable and brighter than they were made to think. They are able to escape from those constraining beliefs, change their fate, challenge assumptions, and achieve what they've always wanted. Winners are the people with the insight and guts to examine the beliefs they were raised with, to continually question the opinions of others, to make their own self-assessment, to challenge others' assumptions, and to decide for themselves what they can and can't do.

Maybe there's a reason why the word "lie" is in the middle of the word "belief"—and this holds true for the academic as well as the personal and business arenas. For example, I remember learning that it was Paul Revere who alerted the Patriots that the British were coming. Didn't you learn that, too? I remember my junior high school history teacher telling us all that Paul Revere madly galloped through the streets yelling, "The British are coming! The British are coming!" Why would I ever question that fact? It's even commemorated in Longfellow's poem, "The Midnight Ride of Paul Revere."

Well, my belief was changed years later when I was writing a speech, and wanted to make a historical reference. Researching the Paul Revere story, I learned that it was not Paul Revere alone who made that famous ride; there were many involved in spreading the word. Supposedly, William Dawes, Joseph Warren, and Israh Bissell, to name a few, were also galloping around delivering the message to alert their neighbors. Don't get me wrong, I understand that "Listen my children and ye shall hear...the midnight ride of Israh Bissell" doesn't rhyme, nor does it make for particularly good copy. However, what's going on? True, the name "Revere" works so much better with the word "hear," but does poetic license permit tampering with history?

Of course, this incident was inconsequential in my life. It didn't damage or affect me in any way. However, it does serve as an example of some of the commonplace things that we were made to believe, which, upon closer scrutiny, turn out to be lacking or untrue.

However, let us go back to those untruths that are more personal in nature—those untruths that can affect you deeply for the rest of your life; those untruths that can influence what you think of yourself, your aspirations, your plans, your expectations, your hopes, and your dreams.

Winners make certain that what they have come to believe, especially about themselves, is self-created, positive, encouraging, and nonrestrictive. Winners challenge assumptions and often make up their own rules. Winners empower themselves. When someone tells a winner, "You can't do that, " the winner questions it, asking "Why not?" When someone tells a winner, "You'll never make that happen," the winner thinks, "Watch me!" Winners take these admonishments as personal challenges. Winners feel that one of the greatest delights and gratifications in life comes from doing things other people say just can't be done. Yes, winners hear the assumptions others make, and then set out to challenge them.

As a speaker, I love to hear how members of my audience have done the supposedly impossible. One gal recently shared how she challenged her manager's assumption that January was the worst sales month of the year, and sold six times as many ads as anyone else in the company. At a recent seminar, a newcomer to a company got up to tell how he was asked to find a noteworthy keynote speaker for his company conference on a meager budget. He told how much pleasure he got out of convincing a famous baseball player to give the opening address well within budget, and with the press at hand. He proudly shared how he was applauded for not only arranging an evening of high impact but also for creating an advertising opportunity that would have cost the company big bucks.

Instances like this happen all the time to everyday people. They happen to people who are not afraid to make their own self-assessment as to what they can and cannot do. They happen to people who challenge assumptions. They happen to winners. As Elbert Hubbard (writer, entrepreneur, editor, and businessman) once said, the world is moving so fast these days that the person who says it can't be done is generally interrupted by another person who is in the midst of doing it.

Winners approach their work and their plans with fewer preconceived notions than most. I recall hearing a story about Thomas Edison, who was known for embarking on his work without preconceived notions. Before Edison would hire anyone to work with him, he wanted to make certain that they had that same trait. History has it that Edison (I'll probably eventually learn that it was Alexander Graham Bell) had a practice of inviting the potential job candidate over for a bowl of soup. If his guest salted the soup before tasting it, Edison eliminated him immediately from the running. You see, Edison didn't want anyone working with him who assumed anything, even if it was simply the notion that most soups need salting.

To start getting rid of any faulty and restrictive beliefs that might be holding you back, do what winners do:

1. *First, recognize the fact that you may have been made to believe things about your own capabilities that can be untrue.* Understand that those beliefs may be keeping you from getting where you want to go.

2. *Make a conscious effort to fight any negative explanatory habits that you may be harboring.* Winners give themselves credit for things that go well, and in fact expect things to go well. Winners think that good is the norm and bad is the exception. Losers tend to think in reverse. Most losers think that if something good happens to them, it was a fluke. But if something bad happens, it was inevitable — it was the way things go, it is the story of their life.

3. *Fight the clichés and go for it.* Realize that many parents, well-meaning relatives, and business associates, perhaps to protect you against life's disappointments, may have planted a seed in your mind that made you think that you were not bright enough, savvy enough, or astute enough to venture out. Many of you perhaps remember your parents giving you that multiple-choice question when you did something a little

brazen, "Hey, are you stupid or what?" Wasn't choosing between those options demoralizing?

Winners take chances. They take risks. They realize that in this age of rapid change, complexity, and upheaval, playing it safe doesn't provide any greater security than taking risks. Business guru Peter Drucker said, "People who don't take risks generally make about two big mistakes a year. People who do take risks generally make about two big mistakes a year."

Many of us were conditioned from early on to play it safe, go with the flow, and not make waves. I recall my mother telling me, "Don't do that; something might happen." "Don't go there; something might happen." "Don't think that way; something might happen." Thank goodness, I never listened to her. Can you imagine going through life with nothing ever happening?

Many of us were programmed to accept mediocrity, to avoid taking chances, to stay on the straight-and-narrow and not to stray from the path. I know that the litany of phrases intended to protect me from disappointment in life and "realistically" re-adjust my dreams still ring loudly in my ears. I bet they ring loudly in your ears as well. I was told that:

- You can't have your cake and eat it too.

- If it looks too good to be true, it probably is.

- If it can go wrong, it most likely will.

- Everything that goes up must come down.

The demoralizing and debilitating list goes on. See if you can fill in the blanks.

- Look before you _____.
- Leave well enough _____.
- Let sleeping dogs _____.
- Keep both feet on the _____.
- Keep your nose to the _____.
- Keep your head above _____.
- Read the handwriting on the _____.

Truthfully, it's hard to do all that at once, especially since you can…Never let 'em see you _____! I was reminded—perhaps you were, too—that if I went astray, I would wind up:

- Between a rock and a _____.
- Between the devil and the _____.
- Up a creek without a _____.

I was cautioned—and maybe you were, too—that I could inadvertently

- Cut off my nose to _____.
- Add insult to _____.
- Wind up behind the eight _____.

Because I wasn't:

- The only pebble on the _____,

- The only fish in the _____.

  Over and over again, I heard:

- Don't count your chickens before they_____.
- Don't put the cart before the _____.
- Don't skate on thin _____.
- Don't rock the _____.
- Don't go out on a _____.
- Don't bite off more than you can _____.

And then there was that big don't, that really damaging and damning don't:

DON'T GET YOUR HOPES UP TOO HIGH.

Now that was good advice, wasn't it? Yes, keep those hopes as low as you possibly can! Aim for the pits in life! Go for the gutter!

Now, I know I wasn't the only person who was inundated with those warnings and that type of advice. It's no wonder so many of us go through life thinking:

- It's just the calm before the _____ .
- This is just too good to be _____.
- Life's a bitch, and then you _____.

Please don't misunderstand me. For the most part, to reiterate, these sayings are drilled into us by well-intentioned people trying to shield us from life's let-downs and disappointments. However, the damage they cause us, the fear they create in us, the mediocrity they perpetuate, and the dreams they stifle are pitiful, lamentable, and appalling.

Winners go for it. They take calculated risks. Neil Simon said, "If no one ever took risks, Michelangelo would have painted the Sistine floor." Yes, winners know that especially if they were not born with a silver spoon in their mouths—taking a chance, venturing out, is the only way they will change their fate. Winners question the beliefs they were handed. Winners question others' assessment of their ability. They know the world would have never been conquered by Attila the Average, Alexander the Bland, Peter the Passive, or Ivan the Dull. They understand that even the lowly turtle has to stick his head out to move.

4. *Evaluate the people you spend time with, because friends tend to share the same beliefs. Are your friends winners or losers?* Make every effort to surround yourself with supportive, positive, action-oriented people who have plans and goals for a great future. Winners look to the future with hope; losers look to the past with regret. Remember, the thing that counts most in your hunt for happiness is choosing the right hunting partners.

We can't choose our parents or our family, but we can choose our friends and our employers. Winners know that negative thinking is not contagious; it's epidemic. They understand that there are toxic people in the world who can poison them and kill their dreams. They avoid these people like the plague— because they know that these people *are* the plague.

Right now, make two lists of the people in your circles, one personal and one professional. Then go back and look at each name. Put a plus (+) or a minus (–) next to each one. Those who are positive, supportive, encouraging, and optimistic get the plus. Those who are negative, unhelpful, discouraging, and pessimistic get the minus. Now, commit to spending less time with—and, if possible, even avoiding—the minuses, and spending more time with the pluses. This is a simple step that is often difficult to take, but is essential in positioning yourself to win. We are defined by our friends. Yes, we are who we hang with. Who do you hang with?

5. *Start a new trend: Believe in yourself.* Sales legend Tom Hopkins said that learning to believe in yourself encourages others to do the same. Remember, belief turns into behavior. What do you believe about you?

Chapter

4

Winning Principle

Winners Make Time Work for Them

Some say these are the good times; some say these are the bad times. Some say these are the right times; some say these are the wrong times. Winners understand that— good times, bad times, right times, wrong times—these are the only darn times they've got, and they know how to make the best of them. Winners know that these *are* the good old days; *these* are the days of their lives.

I was talking with one of my clients about using time productively and how some people never learn that art. He told me that several months ago, after losing a considerable amount of weight, he happened to put on an old jacket, which now happily fit him. As he was checking it out in the mirror, he stuck his hands in his pockets to find a ticket stub for a pair of shoes that he had dropped off for repair at a shoemaker's in March of 1997. He checked his closet and confirmed that the shoemaker must still have those brown loafers.

The following day coming home from work, he decided to try to find the shoemaker. Amazed that it was still in business and not replaced by a 7-Eleven, he parked and went in expecting to find a new owner. To his surprise, the same shoemaker from years back greeted him warmly and said that business was still very good. My client, a bit embarrassed, explained the situation, produced the stub, and asked if by any remote chance his loafers were still around. The shoemaker took the stub, shuffled off to the back room, and returned about 10 minutes later announcing, "Yes, I still have those shoes!" Incredulous, my client then asked the shoemaker what he owed him for the repair. The shoemaker looked down at the shoes for a moment and then turned to my client saying, "You owe me nothing yet; they won't be ready till next Friday."

Time—we try to save it, keep it, make it, cherish it, and use it wisely. Time—we try *not* to waste it, squander it, lose it, or kill it. Time—it supposedly heals all wounds, marches on, flies, waits for no man, and is the same as money.

It seems that technology has not really given us more time; instead it has just allowed us to do more each day with our time. In fact, many people today are so pressed for time that they are caught up in a vortex. They spin from thing to thing, staying in constant motion and trying to do as much as possible in a single day. For people like this, their existence has become like a crazy video game where their responses have to get faster and faster and where the game gets more nerve-racking and complex by the minute. Soon, they quit or shut down because the game becomes too overwhelming.

Many people's lives are just like that. They run around like mad seemingly doing so much but never really accomplishing anything. They think that time management is about efficiency, trying to get as much done as possible in the shortest amount of time. However, winners know that time management really has much more to do with effectiveness than efficiency. Though using time wisely is important, using time to do the right things is even more important.

Actually, I have discovered that one of the most significant distinctions between winners and losers has little to do with the actual amount of work they do, but with the actual amount of *smart* work they do. Therefore, to assure you are working smart, understand some of the principles winners follow, and then incorporate them into your personal action plan.

1. *Winners commit to* making *time for what they want to do.* They know they won't *find* time. The best time or ideal time will not materialize. Therefore, winners *make* time for what they most enjoy doing. They keep handy a list of the things they love to do. Then, they make sure they are actually getting around to doing at least some of them. Winners know that balance gives one perspective, and perspective is critical for long-lasting success. Working toward those future goals is critical. But winners don't forget to take time to live, enjoy, and prosper in their current everyday lives.

2. *Winners actually schedule downtime to simply chill out—alone.* Yes, winners set time aside to wander around, play solitaire, browse through a magazine, go to a museum, take a long bath, and so on. Everyone needs a "vedge ledge," and winners also know that the greatest business ideas happen outside the work realm. Setting some time aside everyday for yourself can prove to be a powerful tonic in today's frenzied world. Rest and recreation are essential elements of the restorative and rejuvenating rhythm of life. It's not smart to run any machine until it breaks down, and the human machine is no exception.

3. *Winners tackle small problems before they grow into bigger ones.* Winners know that the longer a problem exists without being addressed, the more expensive and time consuming it will be to fix. Though the inclination may be to wait and see if it will work itself out, winners don't count on that happening.

4. *Winners are aware that* **considering** *problems and* **worrying** *about them are two different things.* They know that consideration is productive while worrying is pointless.

5. *Winners try to live better and better.* Towards that goal, winners try to find *satisfaction* in their daily lives rather than constantly waiting for that next vacation, that next big break, that next grand party, or retirement. Winners, whether consciously or not, are always asking themselves, "Am I better off today than I was yesterday?" If the answer is "no," they make every concerted effort to make things better. Yes, winners like to feel that every day gets better in some way. Winners know that it's only possible to live happily on a day-to-day basis. While they plan for tomorrow, they know that deferring today's happiness for tomorrow's can lead only to disappointment. Most winners have a goal to have as much pleasure every day as possible.

6. *Winners know how to fight procrastination.* Remember procrastination has many different causes: monotony, fear, perfectionism, boredom, unclear goals, and so on. If procrastination starts creeping into their day,

winners try to identify the reasons behind it. After identifying the cause of procrastination, winners make a mental appointment with themselves. Before that appointment, they jot down the steps needed to avoid further procrastination and to confront the task at hand. This process often helps to clear the screen and keep things moving.

7. *Winners are flexible enough with their time so that they can act quickly when a good idea comes to mind.* Winners know that the fire can quickly smolder unless some immediate follow-through takes place. To make sure the idea gets realized, they discuss it with someone or write down its key points in a memo to be circulated. Calvin Coolidge said, "You cannot do everything at once, but you can do something at once." When a good idea has germinated, it's a perfect time to do something at once.

8. *Winners do not get bogged down.* Winners get rid of any unnecessary procedures and needless red tape. From time to time, they evaluate the processes and systems they have in place. If they can't pinpoint a direct advantage of a currently required procedure, they work hard at trying to eliminate it from their repertoire.

9. *Winners know the parameters of their job and don't waste precious time duplicating other people's work.* This doesn't mean that they don't assist others when appropriate; it just means they have a good pulse on

what they should be doing with their time and what
others should be doing with theirs as well.

10. *Winners take time to organize their time.* Winners make
time to for time management. They have some type of
organizer and use it religiously. In their Palm Pilot, Day
Timer, or Week at a Glance calendar, they enter everything they need to do on a given day, including dropping the kids off at basketball practice, going to the post
office, and so on. Also, they use their organizational system to write down a task so they can forget about it until
they have to deal with it later. In essence, their organizer becomes a portion of their mind, so they can
unburden and free up real head space to handle other
tasks. An organizer also serves as a good reference if
they find themselves with simply not enough hours in
the day to accomplish what needs to be done. By examining their organizing tool, they can easily decipher
patterns of wasted times, unnecessary errands, or ineffi-
cient planning. Additionally, winners tend to have four
lists next to each day on their organizational calendar— **to buy, to call, to do, to think about.**

11. *Winners give themselves **thinking** time that's separate
from their working time.* When working, however,
winners avoid spending an inordinate amount of time
on something they're stuck on. Instead, they turn to
another project, and then return to the more difficult
one when they have time to reboot.

12. *Winners stay focused.* Though winners know how to be flexible, they also understand the importance of focus. That delicate balance takes practice but must be developed. It's easy to get distracted by every crisis that pops up. Winners know that they can't effectively be two places at once. They're not afraid to shut their office door or have their calls held for a designated period of time.

13. *Winners try to act on every item the first time they see it, hear it, or read it.* Winners know that paper is like plaque and it seems to multiply overnight. If they don't brush it away, flush it out, or floss it, that office plaque will soon take over. Therefore, winners make the trash can one of their closest and dearest friends. They know that being a saver is the single greatest cause of disorganization. It's been said that the average person spends six weeks a year just looking for things they can't find in their office.

14. *Winners do not create busy work to avoid doing what needs to be done.* Winners invest the most sweat in what generates the most results. They save questionably productive tasks for their spare time and are indeed interested in that ROTI (Return on Time Invested).

15. *Winners control their e-mail.* Though undoubtedly e-mail is a godsend in many situations, it can also be a curse. On the conservative side, e-mail now eats up on the average of an hour per day. Probably 6 out of 10 e-mail messages are spam or a waste of time. Addition-

ally, much precious time is lost in trying to interpret the tone of e-mails. Winners do not give their e-mail address out indiscriminately and they allocate a specified time to check through those messages, deleting anything that seems questionable. Anyone who truly needs to reach them will be in touch again.

16. *Winners keep a not-to-do list.* Even winners occasionally repeat mistakes. How often have you agreed to do something, done it, and then said "I'm never doing that again"? Then, a few months later, you forget your declaration and do the same thing over again. This can refer to anything—from covering the backside of negligent coworkers to taking care of your neighbor's albino frogs while they vacation. The point is, let experience work for you. Do as winners do: Write down what you don't want to ever do again, keep that list handy, and check it from time to time as a reminder.

17. *Winners help others prioritize so they can work better themselves.* When assigned a must-do project that overwhelms their current workload, winners say something like, "I want to do that job for you and I want to do a great job at it. Therefore, of all the things I'm now doing, tell me what you want me to stop doing so that I have time to dedicate to this?"

18. *Winners avoid phone tag, which takes a good deal of time.* Winners assume they will get voice mail nearly every time they make a phone call today. Therefore, they take a moment up front to plan a message that's

brief and clear with the right details. Doing this increases their odds of getting what they need. And, if the party they are trying to reach is in, all the better, as that message planning will help to expedite the call.

19. *Winners are not stingy with their time when it counts—* and it counts in important relationships. Yes, winners know that time is positively correlated with love. On the personal front, if you feel that someone doesn't love you, chances are you feel that way because they are not giving you enough of their time. That concept translates into business as well. Picking and choosing who to spend time with is critical. Just remember that no one on their deathbed utters, "I only wish that I spent more time working at the office."

20. *Winners ground themselves with solid principles so they don't get diverted from their goals by trends or current crazes.* Winners know that the first step in time management is to establish their values in life. In the comic strip *Calvin and Hobbes,* Calvin's history teacher says, "If there are no questions class, we'll now move on to the next chapter." To this Calvin replies, "I have a question. What is the point of human existence?" The teacher, a bit perplexed and annoyed, explains, "Calvin, I meant that I would take any questions about the history subject at hand." "Oh," Calvin responds. "Well, frankly, I'd like to have my question resolved before I expend any more energy on anything else."

Winners think about the point of their existence. They formulate values based on that and make a conscious effort to spend time doing what will make those values a part of their life.

Winners know that time management has really nothing to do with the clock, but everything to do with organizing, directing, regulating, monitoring, and commanding their involvement in certain events which happen to synchronize with the clock.

Einstein felt that the phrase "time management" was something of an oxymoron. Time moves forward despite circumstances. Time is the one level playing field in life. We all begin each day with the same 24 available hours, 1,440 minutes, 86,400 seconds. Winners know you can't really manage time; you can only control the events within a given period of time. Though you can make use of time—be it sitting at your desk to outline a speech you are to deliver or shooting wads of balled-up paper into your trash can—the seconds will continue to click on.

Winners know how to live life with no intermissions. Winners know that wasting time turns out to be the most pricey extravagance of them all.

Chapter
5

Winning Principle

Winners Move Others to Action

Let's face it, even the Lone Ranger didn't ride alone. Though you may consider yourself an extremely resourceful person, more often than not, to bring your plans to fruition, you will require help from others. Yes, for most of us, success requires an ensemble performance, and it is indeed difficult to maintain momentum if all the players are not working in concert.

We need others—not just because we're social animals by nature, but also because we rarely can do it all alone. Yes, we need others to help us make things happen, we need others to work *with* us and *for* us. We need others to help execute our ideas, to encourage our projects, to support our endeavors, and to do the tasks we need them to do. Therefore, in the work arena or on the home front, knowing how to help move others along, knowing how to fan that motivational flame within others, knowing how to get others to do as you want them to do, is a vital part of winning.

One of my clients is an elderly gentleman who ruled his company with the proverbial iron hand and hollow heart. His concept of getting others to perform centered on *fear.* I recall during one particularly difficult training session, he popped in to see how "his people" were progressing. After observing someone stumble over a sales role-play exercise, he yelled out "Hey, how long have you been working for my company...not counting tomorrow?" Clearly, his tactic to get others to perform was based on threats and intimidation. Clearly, he had no idea that public criticism alienates everyone. I immediately realized that before I could continue working with his "beaten" staff, I would have to see if *he* was retrainable. I had to see if he could change his attitude. I had to see if he had the ability and interest to learn what really makes people perform. I had to see if he could be motivated to change his leadership style.

This scenario reminded me of something that winners seem to innately realize: The most difficult part of working with people is, indeed, *working with people.* Yes, winners recognize that fact, but they also know how to do it. Winners know how to get the most out of others, how to help others perform at their peak, and they also know that it has little to do with intimidation or fear. Helping people to perform is a challenge that winners know how to conquer.

Even with all the new management concepts floating around today, there are still many managers and executives out there who believe, "Hell, when I hire them, they should be motivated to perform and stay motivated. That's part of the job." Yes, and the tooth fairy lives.

Of course, winners try to load the decks in their favor. Before offering someone the job, they usually test potential hires to get a better handle on them. Unfortunately, though there are many revealing instruments out there that pinpoint personality types, psychological profiles, and one's overall stability, all these tests share a common flaw: None accurately predicts one's ability to self-motivate and perform well on the job. Since some people audition very well, but go down hill from there, the lack of an accurate self-motivational testing tool for companies has been extremely costly.

Inspiring others to perform has been a problem that man has wrestled with since the beginning of time. The most basic and first motivator along these lines was indeed that simple thing called fear. In essence, the caveman with the biggest club was the best or, shall we say, the most influential, inspirer in the entire group.

Today, many inept people, and not just those from the old school, still use fear thinking it will move others along. "If you don't get this important account, you're done here." "We're having a sales contest, and the winners get to keep their jobs." "If you don't clean up your room, you're grounded." The words from the powerful movie *Glengarry Glen Ross* still ring in my ears, "First place in sales, you get a Cadillac. Second place, you get a set of steak knives. Third place, you get fired."

Now, fear as an inspirational tool is not entirely worthless. In fact, it may indeed work initially. However, it has proven to work only for a short time. Fear, used to incite better performance, has four downfalls: 1) It is external — it comes from outside — while true motivation, as I noted earlier, must come from within; 2) It is negative; 3) Those working under its threat soon become numb to it, rendering it ineffective; and 4) Though chastisement and punishment may work to eliminate specific unwanted behaviors, employee reactions to it are erratic and unpredictable. In other words, though fear may prevent unacceptable behaviors in one arena, it usually encourages and justifies an equally unacceptable, or even worse, behavior in another area. As an inspirer, fear is simply risky business, and does not create an ultimately productive and positive work environment.

As the human race got more sophisticated, a new element was added to the fear package: It was called the *carrot*, the reward, the prize. Interestingly enough, however, that too has proven to have an unreliable and limited inspirational shelf life. You see, after a while, the prize proves not to be enough. In fact, the prize has to keep getting bigger and better to have any real significance.

In other words, though salary increases, larger commissions, bonuses, shorter work hours, fringe benefits, and spiff vacations may be typical rewards that are always welcomed, such rewards are soon construed by employees as part of the job. If employees don't get their spiffs, they get ticked off; and ticked off employees will not give you their all.

Now, I am not intimating that one shouldn't provide employees with these types of rewards. It's just that winners don't fool themselves into thinking that such rewards will ensure or inspire peak performance.

Sure, those extras will most likely enhance a company's recruitment efforts, and that benefit can't be dismissed. However, winners know that those prizes will not guarantee employees who will work with conscientiousness, self-discipline, initiative, loyalty, dependability, energy, and enthusiasm.

In understanding how to move employees positively and productively, there are four words that are important to define:

Ability—refers to what one is capable of doing.

Motivation— refers to what one will actually do.

Attitude—refers to the frame of mind one has while doing what they do.

Potential—is a nice word that refers to the fact that nothing's been done yet!

Now, don't get me wrong, I'm not down on "potential" as a concept. I know that helping to develop someone's potential is a wonderful thing that many winners do. I know that helping others to grow, investing in people, coaching, mentoring, and so on, are powerful and magnanimous undertakings. However, I have found out that winners know when they should take the time to develop another's potential and when they shouldn't. Winners know when they can take the chance that the potential they see will turn into ability and top performance, and when they can't take that chance.

Putting potential aside, however, winners know that when their success depends on the performance of others; they have to be able to inspire peak performance in those who may have difficulty mustering up their own inspiration. Yet inspiring others is not an easy task. In fact, managing others in general has often been compared to working in a cemetery. In other words, you may have many people under you, but—no one's listening.

So when trying to encourage peak performance in others, the dollars, prizes, and perks are simply not enough. The fact of the matter is that people are motivated to perform when a certain working environment exists—and that environment is not really a physical one, but more of a psychological one. That environment is one in which the **intangible** needs of an employee are met. In that manner, it's an **environment** that proves to be the catalyst for top performance and on-the-job effectiveness.

Over the years, many people such as the well-known and brilliant Maxwell Maltz (not a psychologist by training, but a plastic surgeon) have written about intangible human needs. Authors as diverse as Wayne Dyer, Gloria Steinem, Zig Ziglar, and Anthony Robbins recognize the following needs that, alone or in combination, serve as chief motivators. Most of them are intangible.

1. Affection—a yearning to be liked.
2. Acceptance—a longing to belong.
3. Ego—a sense of having a good opinion of yourself.
4. Recognition—a wish for admiration by others.
5. Excellence—a desire to succeed, perhaps triumph.
6. Greed—a want for more than a fair share, self-indulgence.
7. Liberty—a craving for independence and freedom.
8. Power—a yen for dominance, control, and authority.
9. Privacy—an urge for personal space.
10. Security—a need for protection from threat.

Winners know that truly inspired people perform because someone has made it feel good to perform. Someone has created an environment that makes them feel rewarded in a special, meaningful way—by providing one or several of those intangibles to them. To keep these intangibles rolling in, most people will go out of their way to please. Also, of course (as Pavlov showed us), we tend to repeat the actions that are rewarded.

Though each person may be moved by different intangibles, here are 27 ways winners create the psychological environment that covers most of them, thus offering the rewards that encourage people to work at peak-performance levels. See how well you help others do their best for you:

1. *Winners praise frequently; in fact, if you can't stroke and praise, you'll have a tough time inspiring others to do anything.* Ken Blanchard's advice to "catch people doing something good" is critical.

2. *Winners praise in front of others as often as possible.* Praise in front of others delivers 10 times more bang for the buck.

3. *When winners praise, they praise as specifically as they would reprimand.* In life, reprimands tend to be specific and praise tends to be general. "The figures in this report don't add up. Besides that, it's sloppy, hard to read, and your conclusions make no sense to me." That is specific reprimand. "You did a good job. Way to go!" That's general praise—too general.

4. *Winners, on an ongoing basis, tell their employees how important they are to the end result.* For many, being needed is motivating, and is often tied into acceptance, ego, recognition, and affection.

5. *Winners keep employees informed.* They include them in the decision-making process as often and as appropriate as possible.

6. *Winners keep information flowing.* They know that those who hoard information are insecure individuals with low self-confidence, who need to withhold information in order to bolster their own power.

7. *Winners always tell the troops the truth.*

8. *Winners make sure that others in the company, including the top brass, commend the achievements of all employees.*

9. *Winners encourage input from their team.* They inform them that their advice will be asked for and often used.

10. *Winners are direct when communicating with their team and require the team to be direct back.* For example, I know a sales manager who always asks her team to specifically list the steps they plan to take in order to reach their projected sales numbers for the month. It's about specifics.

11. *Winners clearly define the employee's decision-making range.* Empowerment must still have parameters.

12. *Winners help their team win by delineating to the staff what's expected of them.* This is done not just in terms of project objectives, sales goals, or dollar volume, but also in terms of performance procedures as well as follow-through techniques and practices.

13. *Winners give their teams and employees success goals, not just performance goals.* For example, recently one of my clients had his employees call sales leads back after normal work hours. It was a night dedicated to reconnecting with interested prospects. The team leader gathered everyone together with plenty of phone hook ups and plenty of pepperoni pizza. They went to work and spent three hours carrying out the evening goal: Making follow-up calls. It would have been much more productive, however, if instead the mission for each person was to get three firm follow-up appointments for the next week. In other words, the troops were given a performance goal, rather than a success goal. Though the performance goal reaped some results, the success goal would have expedited the mission and reaped even greater rewards.

14. *Winners make sure their team members are well aware of the company's situation, objectives, and expectations.* Then, based on that information, they have the team members set their own goals. If you set the goals for your team, they are your goals; if they set them, they are their goals. We tend to rally around what we participate in formulating.

15. *Winners are involved with their teams.* They have a strong presence and high profile with them. As many have said, you can pretend to care, but you can't pretend to be there. Winners are there to listen, talk, and help. Unfortunately many executives engage in something called a *flight from dependency.* Yes, quite often managers do anything they can to actually remove themselves or distance themselves from the staff. They do this because the concept that they are depending on these people to deliver makes them terribly uncomfortable and uneasy. So they disappear from the scene. They make themselves scarce. They isolate themselves from their staff. Unfortunately, this absence does not translate to the employee as a sign of trust; instead it comes off as a lack of interest and caring.

16. *Winners compensate fairly.* People can only do their best **on** the job if they are not worried about their day-to-day survival **off** the job.

17. *Winners structure rewards to benefit the employee's immediate family.* In that way, the family will be more tolerant of those occasional late nights, unpredictable hours, and last-minute meetings.

18. *Winners promote the staff's physical health.* Company-sponsored team sports, lunchtime aerobics, health club memberships, and so on, energize people—and energized people work better. Additionally, activities like this create camaraderie, a sense of belonging, and more team spirit.

19. *Winners give their employees a venue to toot their own horn.* Madonna recently echoed Mae West's words, "If you don't toot your own horn, it means your battery is dead." Providing an outlet that enables all members of your team to boost their individual egos is critical in creating this psychological environment that promotes top performance. Have one team member teach the group how to accomplish something he is particularly good at, or have a team member write an article on a recent predicament or challenge that she handled with finesse and success.

20. *Winners provide a work environment where fun and surprises exist—a movie afternoon, the funniest joke contest, the baby-picture guessing game, and so on.* This may sound hokey, but it has proven to bring a great deal to the workplace.

21. *Winners, from time to time, give immediate rewards for the accomplishment of mini goals.* For example, award a prize to the person who conducted the most product demonstrations this week, or provide a reward to the person who sold more maintenance agreements, or give a gift to the person who came in under budget on the current project phase. This process helps develop good habits and serves to spur people on.

22. *Winners provide people with an opportunity for self-enhancement.* Dale Carnegie courses, Toastmasters, financial-planning seminars, and time-management programs can enhance both one's on-the-job and off-the-job life.

23. *Winners demonstrate pride and trust in their employees by having them represent the company at national conventions, dinner meetings, or industry events.*

24. *Winners make sure their team knows that risk taking will be rewarded.* As Tom Peters said, "Today the greatest risk is not taking one."

25. *Winners adhere to the policies and procedures that are established.* For example, what's the system for expense reimbursement? Who makes out the request? In how many days can employees expect to get their money back? Without systems that are adhered to, you have no structure, morale starts deteriorating, and the bottom-line suffers. Most people are very sensitive. They work within a pattern range of reactions. They find it hard to separate one thing from another. For example, if they were responsible for buying supplies or refreshments for a meeting and were not reimbursed promptly, they might doubt the company's solvency. Such doubts will unfortunately get transferred on to other employees and eventually reach the customer.

26. *Winners know that people do unto others as they themselves are done unto.* Therefore, they never forget that those who are not well-served do not serve others well. Winners know that it must start at the top.

27. *Winners make sure their team has B'HAGs.* James Collins and Jerry Porras from Stanford University noted that when studying outstanding companies, it wasn't necessarily the charisma or inspirational magic that the leaders wielded that made it all happen; it was

the B'HAGs. B'HAG is an acronym for Big, Hairy, Audacious Goal. Now, I know that all companies have goals. Some have short-term goals; some have long-term goals. I was with a company the other day who's short-term goal was to stay in business long enough to make long-term goals. However, there is a difference between having goals and becoming committed to a huge, potentially difficult and daunting challenge — like climbing a mountain, partaking in the Marine Corps Marathon, or producing the largest profits.

To give others an idea of a B'HAG, Porras and Collins cited JFK's bold goal in the early 1960s of placing a man on the moon before the end of the decade. That was quite brazen, since the technology did not exist at that point to enable that to happen. At General Electric, a B'HAG was announced to its employees: To become number one or number two in every market it served. Sam Walton was known for setting B'HAGs that still serve to inspire his employees long after he's gone.

Yes, a goal of that magnitude engages people; it grabs them in a way that results in high focus and high energy. It breeds determination and can result in amazing achievements.

So, winners know that they don't need a mission statement or a list of goals that's pages long. All they need to do is think of what Sir Edmund Hillary supposedly said when he set off to climb Mount Everest: "We're going to the top!"

So ask yourself:

- Do I want to get to the top?
- Since it is not a solo act, do I have others to help me?
- Am I giving others what they need to get me where I want to go?

Winners know that others perform when their intangible needs are met. Winners create the psychological environment that meets those needs. Winners stay winners with the help of others. Evaluate what you are doing to get others to help you.

Chapter
6

Winning Principle

Winners Have a Sense of Urgency

I'm about 180 degrees away from anything to do with cowboys, rodeos, and ropin'. So I knew I was headed for a new experience when my clients from Calgary told me that I would be delivering my seminar in the theater on the grounds of the Calgary rodeo. As it turned out, the facility was fantastic—no dirt on the ground but instead stadium-style seats with foldaway desks and a stage that was a speaker's dream. After completing a segment in my program about the importance of having a sense of urgency, one of the attendees told me a story about a reporter who was interviewing one of the most famous of all rodeo cowboys here in Calgary.

The reporter, shocked to learn that this cowboy was 62 years old and still riding, expressed his amazement by saying, "I can't believe that at 62 you have the stamina and dexterity to work the rodeo circuit." "Hell," answered the cowboy, "that ain't nothing. My Pa is 81, and he's still riding in the rodeo." Now the reporter was even more intrigued, "You've got to be kidding. I'd really like to meet your Pa and interview him for this story as well." The cowboy shook his head and said, "No can do. You see today Pa is standing up for Grandpa in Edmonton. Grandpa is 100 years old and he's getting married this very morning." Now incredulous, the reporter replied, "Wait a minute. You mean to tell me that you have a grandfather who is 100 years old and wants to get married?" "Hell, Mister," said the cowboy, "You got it all wrong. Grandpa don't want to get married, Grandpa's got to get married."

Urgency can be created by others or it can be self-created. In fact, it has been said that there are three types of urgency: conceived (imagined), perceived (real), and deceived (tricked or duped).

Now grandpa's urgency might have been more the deceived type than anything else, but it served nevertheless to move him. Though I can make no assessment as to whether grandpa was a winner or a loser, I have noted that winners, people who make things happen in this world, all seem to share a sense of urgency. That sense of urgency not only serves to move them along but it also serves to move others along as well.

Yes, winners all seem to have an urge to want to do it now. They tend to be impatient with themselves as well as with others. Even if the project can wait, even if most likely nothing will change if the work gets started tomorrow instead of today, even if the matter is not pressing—winners are the folks who want to get on with it or have it done now…right now.

I recall working for a developer from Southern California who hired me during the second building phase of a high-density town house community near Princeton, New Jersey. My role not only included training and inspiring his sales team, but I was also to consult with him on marketing issues. Early one Monday morning at the weekly meeting, my client requested my opinion of the sales center that was erected long before I entered the scene. He wanted my feedback in terms of its curb appeal, interior customer comfort, lighting, appropriateness, and impact of the visual displays, and so on.

I commented that everything seemed fine except that the double-wide trailer, which served as the sales and information center, could have been situated in a much better place within the community, so as to lead the customers who turned off the main road past some of the amenities en route. I explained that if it was located on the other side of the main entrance and a bit further into the community, those driving through could readily see the lifestyle value here, and immediately this community would differentiate itself from all others going up in this area at this time. Jim, the company president, intently listened as I spoke. By 1:30 that afternoon, the double-wide trailer was moved to the suggested new site. It all happened so fast that when we returned from lunch I thought I was delusional.

Not only was this particular community a success, but everything Jim touches turns out profitably. Among other things, he's a man who has been blessed with that sense of urgency. When Jim wants it done, it is done—then and there.

I have found that you can be brilliant and skilled, but without that sense of urgency your achievements and successes just won't match up to the accomplishments of those who may be far less intelligent or capable but possess that wonderful sense of "now." No matter what your intelligence level or talent may be, no matter how smart or savvy you are, if you want to win you must develop a sense of urgency.

Here are five main reasons why a sense of urgency is important:

1. *There is a positive correlation between quitters and poor starters.* In other words, those who tend to abandon a project or give up on it easily usually were not those who were anxious or eager to begin the job in the first place.

2. *We live in a fast and impatient world.* The future is colliding with the present at unprecedented rates of speed. And the old cliché about being in the right place at the right time has been changed: today, you have to be in the right place *ahead* of the right time. Fast has come to mean good. Fast is the way. We have:

   Fast foods

   Quick relief

   Instant pudding

   Rapid transit

   Speedy Alka-Seltzer

   Rush orders

   Fleeting romances

   Brief encounters

   Kwik Copy

   Sir Speedy

Jiffy Lube and even,

Microwave Minute Rice

Today you have to be fast, faster than your competitor. You have to be quicker in many ways, especially when it comes to being able to provide your customers and clients with information, products, and services. You may be better than the other guy, but if you don't deliver immediacy, you'll soon be out of business. A sense of impatience—a sense of expediency, a sense of urgency in terms of fulfilling orders, launching new products, following up with clients, interpreting and applying research—matters now more than ever before in the history of business.

3. *A sense of urgency helps you use your time to the fullest extent, and in an earlier chapter I discussed how important that is.* Yes, in life, time is the restrictive factor, the limiting issue. The writer Israel Davidson said, "Time is infinitely more precious than money, and there is nothing common between them. You cannot accumulate time, you cannot borrow time, you can never tell how much time you have left in the bank of life. Time is life." Having a sense of urgency can enable you to have a fuller, richer life—quite simply you will be able to accomplish and experience more.

4. *A sense of urgency accelerates one's state of "readiness."* When opportunity is on the horizon it encourages

you to jump in ahead of others. It's been proven that in life one will never get much of anything done unless they do it *before* they're ready to. Being able to jump in, even when not necessarily feeling *ready,* is a step in gaining the competitive advantage as well as part of a visionary leadership attitude. In fact, being first in many cases is even more important than being the best. Few remember the second person to fly solo across the Atlantic Ocean. However, the second trip was accomplished in less time with a plane that consumed much less fuel than the one Lindberg piloted during his famous flight. But Lindberg was first! Lindberg jumped in before the other guy!

Most people wait to feel a firm sense of that elusive "readiness" before they take action. Winners know that waiting for that feeling can result in missed opportunities as well as a life that is put on hold.

"Readiness" has been defined as the quality or state of being prepared to act promptly, to act immediately. Many people, however, erroneously believe that when you become ready, a green light appears, or a buzzer sounds off indicating that it's appropriate to now proceed.

Winners know that in reality "readiness" is something that usually occurs *after* the fact, not before it. Yes, readiness happens after you start something rather than before you tackle it.

Most often, being in the situation itself makes us get ready, much more so than the preparation for the situation. How many times do people who are given the opportunity to handle a new client, or to advance to a higher position, ask themselves, "Am I really ready for this?" Once in the throes of it all, however, they seem to get ready. At first they may have to work a little harder or perhaps even fake it. But they find out that "readiness" is something that happens along the way. Who is ready? Was I ready to have kids? (You have to be kidding!) Was I ready to travel three to four days a week? (Are you out of your mind?) I got ready when I had to be ready...winners do that, and so can you.

Having a sense of urgency redefines "readiness" and gives you an advantage in all walks of life. Contrary to what your mother told you, all does not come to those who wait, and he who hesitates is not only lost but also forgotten.

5. *The importance of having a sense of urgency can be seen in Parkinson's Law: "Work will expand according to the time you have allotted for it."* So by getting to it now and then by giving yourself *a more pressing timetable* to finish the task, you may actually be making less work for yourself in the long run—and free up time to do other things.

Now, often people have a sense of inner urgency that moves them, personally, along, but how can this be transmitted to others? If your job requires creating urgency in others, your ability to communicate that sense will be critical to your success. Lecturing about it will not do the trick and demanding it will not work either. When valid-sounding excuses are needed to justify delays, today the world of technology has handed them to us on a silver platter. "My computer is down" or "The system crashed" has been used to explain countless urgency failures on the part of employees. On the other hand, showing personal interest in the job you want others to accomplish, monitoring their progress and being available for assistance will invariably make it happen sooner rather than later. Here are some other specific ways that you can communicate that sense of urgency to your team:

1. After project plans have been reviewed, ask the project leader or person responsible to tell you when he plans to *start the project*. Then, request to be contacted once he actually begins the job.

2. Ask the leader for a time estimate as to when the project will be completed.

3. If applicable, discuss what (if anything) the leader might have to stop doing to complete the current task on schedule.

4. Follow up to see that others carry through and reward them for the small steps they accomplish along the way.

5. When meeting on the project, expect promptness from others and be prompt yourself. Promptness is not just a sign of good manners and respect, it is a

demonstration of professionalism and an indication of urgency.

6. Make it your job to clear the roadblocks out of the way. Don't let others be frustrated while waiting for answers, decisions, slow-moving procedures, and red tape. Do your job in such a manner that those under your supervision have no excuses for not getting their job done. Always, keep the ball in their court.

In our carpe momento, or seize the moment, world, having or creating a sense of urgency does not stop here. Winners know that often their biggest challenge is creating a sense of urgency with their customers. Therefore, make certain that you are not unintentionally giving customers a reason to stall. When you say, "Would you like to get together?" or "Can we get together to discuss this?" you allow your prospects to slip out of a commitment and you eliminate that sense of urgency that makes progress happen. Instead, be firm, and be immediate. "We need to meet now," or, "At this point, the essential next step is to get together in the next 48 hours."

Winners know that one of these days usually turns out to be none of these days. Winners know that "someday" is not a day of the week. Winners also know that one of the greatest labor saving strategies of today is unfortunately still mañana.

Even if you already have that innate sense of urgency, you still have to be selective in how you exercise it. You can't possibly have a do-it-now mentality about everything. Prioritizing will indeed come into play, because if everything is equally important, nothing actually becomes important. However, for starters consider taking the following steps to develop a better, saner sense of "now":

- *Understand that working on what has to be done is not nearly as tiring and exhausting as thinking about what has to be done.* Taking that first step will often be your most difficult challenge, but just by getting started you will truly feel better.

- *Don't focus on **all** you have to do to bring the project to completion, or to reach your goal.* Instead, get into the habit of breaking that first step down. Remember you can't "do" a goal; you can only do the behaviors that will lead to that goal. Ask yourself, what is one behavior I can do now that would get me closer to my goal? Not knowing where to start is a main cause for procrastination. Break the project down into a list of baby steps that you can approach one at a time.

- *When you get started on the job, begin by doing something where the results of your efforts can clearly and easily be seen.* If the task is organizing your office, first start by cleaning off the top of your file cabinets—rather than attacking the inside of your file drawers—which would not be seen unless opened. Or if you've been putting off making those calls, enter the names in your palm pilot or day timer so you can check them off once you have made contact. In that way, you can see the results of your work. *Seeing* little successes will encourage you to pursue the less visible and obvious ones.

- *If it can be done in less than five minutes, do it now.* When postponed, the little details of life bog us down and overwhelm us. When we put the little things off, they seem to build in magnitude and importance. Do not turn minor tasks into major ones by avoiding them.

- *Use your energy according to your personal peak times.* Morning is not everyone's best time. Plan to get going on that new project when your energy reaches its daily high point. Commit to finding out when that time is and remember it will be easiest to muster up your energy then.

- *Get organized.* Every day before leaving work, clean off your desk for the next day. No matter what type of person you are (even if you're a creative mastermind), it has been proven that neatness contributes to thought clarity and mitigates that overwhelmed feeling that often prevents us from jumping in and tackling something new. If for no other purpose, clean your desk off for health reasons. Most people don't clean their desks until they're sticking to it! Health professionals say that toilet seats are actually cleaner than most desks. I'm not intimating that you should eat your lunch on your toilet seat, but environmental cleanliness in most cases does lead to thought clarity.

- *Realize that your lack of urgency can come from sheer laziness.* The fact that peanut butter and jelly now comes in one jar confirms my suspicion that most of us are getting lazier. Winners, however, are simply not lazy people. So if you feel that laziness is one of your debilitating issues, before anything else, you'll have to find out whether your brand of laziness is caused by diet, lack of exercise, medication, poor sleep patterns, or from a poor choice in friends and associates whose get up and go kind of petered out and stayed put. Drive is contagious.

  However, do not confuse laziness with loneliness. Maybe you're quite simply the kind of person who needs company to tackle a task. That's okay. If that's the case, you have to get someone to work with you or at the very least elicit the help of an interested coworker or friend to check in with you frequently and discuss your progress.

- *Understand that when we are trying to avoid something we often welcome and even seek out interruption.* So, if you're trying to stir up some urgency in your life, tell your family, friends, and coworkers not to interrupt you for a designated period of time.

- *Every night make a to-do list for the next day.* Many feel that this step alone is therapeutic in creating a feeling of getting started. In any case, it's a sign of maturity, as kids rarely would even consider making a list. Only dorks would be that organized. As a child, I

remember my parents often suggesting that I make a
pro/con list when I had a dilemma. I also remember
hating that idea. Kids don't want lists—nor do they
particularly need lists. As a child, what's important
doesn't have to be written down. However, as we age,
we have more things to remember and issues seem
to become more urgent. As a child, why would I
need to make a note to make a dental appointment?
I hated going to the dentist and besides I had friends
who never brushed their teeth and still had white,
bright smiles. As you get older, you think about
repercussions. I think, "Hell, I better make that dental appointment because now that I can afford lob-
ster I don't want to have to puree it in my Cuisinart
and suck it through a straw."

After you make that one list divide it into two categories. *What I **might** do tomorrow,* and *What I **will** do tomorrow.* If you make only one list, the items will tend to en-
gulf you into shutting down and doing nothing. However,
if you break that one list down into two, and if you make
the will-do list very short, you will be amazed at how much
you actually get done on both lists.

If you find that either you or someone you know could
benefit from a stronger sense of urgency and none of the
above tips serves to get that going, as a last resort, you can
check out the Sharper Image catalogue to see if they are
still selling the Timesis life clock. If they are, buy one. Be
it a gift for yourself or for that person who needs to get

going now, I've found it to be a very effective urgency cre-
ation device. Now, to set the clock you will have to program in some data that will be requested in the directions.
Then based on that input as well as on actuarial tables the
computer in this clock will calculate how long you (or
whoever) have left to live. It will then set itself for the number of days and hours left in life…and then it will start tick-
ing backwards. I guarantee that just watching those
seconds tick off can really create a sense in urgency in anyone with a heartbeat.

Winners know that though we have to treasure our yes-
terdays and daydream our tomorrows, we must live our
todays to the fullest! They know that a sense of urgency is
essential toward accomplishing their goals. They know
that every day is filled with opportunity. Winners don't
want to miss a minute of it.

Chapter

7

Winning Principle

*Winners Know That Positive Mental
Attitude Can Be Highly Overrated*

A positive mental attitude is undoubtedly a characteristic of winners. It's almost a no-brainer that people who are more affirmative, more constructive, more up-beat, and more optimistic are also more likely to be able to see, to be offered, and to capitalize on opportunities better than people who are cynical, skeptical, negative, or contemptuous. Most of us have grown up with stories that demonstrate how important in life a positive mental attitude is.

I recall as a child hearing the story of Cinderella, who kept her positive attitude amidst the horror of her wicked stepmother and her taunting stepsisters. I remember her acceptance of the fact that she could not go to the ball. I recall her bravery in not caving in to the injustice. I marveled at how she kept washing, dusting, and cleaning out the fireplace, still clinging to the hope that, in the end, Dr. Norman Vincent Peale and Dale Carnegie would be right and her positive mental attitude would pay off, save her, and take her away from the mess she was in.

I also remember when she was granted her wish, when she attended the ball, when she danced with the prince, and of course when she lost her glass slipper. I will never forget the crescendo of the story, which always swept me away. Yes, Cinderella's positive mental attitude did, in the final analysis, bring her happiness. That lost slipper was oh-so-fortunately traceable. A dedicated pursuit by the prince to find the mystery woman ensued, and Cinderella's luck stayed with her—as when the Prince tried the slipper on her foot, she wasn't retaining any water. Yes, it fit and they went off together and lived happily ever after.

What a story. What a message. However, winners know it is precisely because of that message that this story is called a fairy tale. Winners know that a positive mental attitude alone is not enough to make any significant change in your life. Winners know that having a positive mental attitude is just the beginning. It alone will never turn your life around, change your current situation, or make your wishes come true. Though it will sure take you through life with a better outlook and a better mood than a negative attitude, winners know that a positive mental attitude alone can't be relied on to make anyone a real winner.

Perhaps you, as I, know plenty of people with effusive personas and positive mental attitudes who are still losers. They talk a good line; they think good thoughts; they're optimistic and upbeat. They have, what I call "the current-day Midas touch." In other words, everything they touch turns into a muffler.

Winners know that though a positive mental attitude is the essential threshold one needs to cross over to get into a winning position; it can be a detriment if it is solely relied on to significantly impact your life and get you where you want to go. Yes, a positive mental attitude can actually hurt you, if:

- You have construed attitude to be cerebral alone and to only manifest itself mentally, not physically.

In other words, you have mastered the fine art of interpreting, thinking, planning, deliberating, and dissecting, but have ignored the appropriate behavioral follow-through.

- You fool yourself into thinking positively about something that doesn't necessarily deserve that designation. "Even though my boss is mean, conniving, heartless, and downright unethical, I'm sure if I look hard enough I'll find some good in her."

- You are so taken with your positive projected attitude that you have confused self-esteem for self-importance and have, along the way, developed a sense of entitlement.

- While embracing your positive attitude, you have gone over the line from confidence to arrogance.

Let's take a look at the first potential pitfall of a positive attitude in the preceding list. Remember, though attitude normally refers to a way of thinking, it has to also manifest itself in behavior to make a significant impact in your life. A positive attitude has to envelope your entire manner—and, your manner involves the physical as well as the mental.

Your positive physical body language reveals quickly to the world your mental condition. For example, in the business world, I see so many potential winners projecting a losing appearance by having a negative stance rather than a positive one. It's more than slouching, and bad posture, however. It's also that positive people are visible, they make their presence known, they are energized by the convictions they have, and that energy radiates and spills forth.

How do you maneuver at meetings or business gatherings? Do you take up space? Do you have a sense of presence? Remember, you don't have to be big to have a presence and be noticed; nor do you have to be loud, aggressive, or dramatic. Think of those superheroes: Superman, Spiderman, Wonder Woman, and Aquaman. Yes, all are larger than life. Look at how they present themselves. They take up space. They stand, legs apart, hands on hips, heads up, chin out. Grandma always said, "Stand straight and tall." She knew that that was the first critical step in projecting a more positive and confident appearance. Being hunched over in the corner of the room, slithering around behind the scenes, or slinking into the meeting and grabbing a seat in the back will not do it. Being an action–oriented person and being thought of as confident, capable, and highly visible tells others about your attitude.

Though it's been stated that the biggest gap in the world is the gap between knowing and doing, winners are positive doers. It's not about being noticed to gain attention for attention's sake; it's about radiating a vibrancy that comes from a powerful, active, upbeat, optimistic source within. Winners think and act positively, definitively, not hesitantly. They have great conviction and energy—both are contagious. Yes, action is needed to win, and winning is like sweat: It's indeed a by-product of activity!

Action makes that good attitude pay off, and in fact, action can even change a bad attitude. It has been agreed upon by many professional therapists that action is the only antidote to stress and despair. Yes, it's a change in behavior that leads to a change in attitude. Losers try to *think* themselves out of a bad mood. Winners know they must *act* themselves out of a bad mood. **How you think does not determine how you act. How you act determines how you think!** Those on a winning path know that, and work with that premise to keep themselves as upbeat as possible.

To change your current situation, to position yourself to win, you must take some type of action! It doesn't always have to be terribly significant, ultimately life changing, or dramatic. For starters, it can even be a hit-and-miss type of action. But you are far better off bumping around out there than moping around in your mind.

So, for starters:

1. Get on the phone and connect with someone you haven't spoken to in a while.

2. Get out there and make it a goal to introduce yourself to someone new every day.

3. Take a different route to work.

4. Dine at a new restaurant or try a new take-out.

5. Change your daily routine in some simple way.

6. Engage in any kind of physical activity (roller blading, dancing, walking, biking) on a routine weekly basis.

7. Take one step every week to do something that will either simplify or better arrange your life.

8. At least one evening during the week, get out of the house to do something that will enrich your life. For example, take a new course, attend a seminar, listen to a lecture series, visit a museum, attend a ballet or concert, join a bridge group, take tap-dancing or Tai Bo lessons.

Next, let us look at the danger that can occur if your positive attitude is contributing to making you think about something in better terms than it deserves. Dreams are good. I encourage everyone to dream. I'm a big dreamer myself. In fact, I remember when I learned that there was no such thing as the Easter Bunny, my secretary could hardly console me. The problem is, however, that often people, due to their positive attitude, formulate dreams that don't match up with their talents or ability to realize them. Of course, though turning a dream into reality does rely on a positive mental attitude and positive motivated action, we must make certain that we don't set ourselves up for frustration and disappointment, and that we don't waste time reaching for something that can and will never happen.

I knew of a great receptionist in a prominent Los Angeles consulting firm who loved to sing. She was a decent vocalist, she certainly knew how to belt-out a song, and she stayed on key. Unfortunately, there was nothing outstanding about her voice, and she certainly was not star material. Her dream was to perform in musical theater on Broadway, and she held those high hopes with an extremely positive attitude in terms of that eventually happening. Her family, seeing her through rose-colored glasses, and feeling a sense of endearment and love towards her, were very supportive and encouraging.

Her family recognized her limits, but they figured, "What's the harm in flattering her? Why should we spoil her dreams?" Yes, in order to spare her feelings, they encouraged her and actually hid the truth from her. She thought she was good and she was good. However, clearly she did not have what it would take to make it—even with all the persistence in the world. She wound up living a confused and frustrating life, fighting to keep a positive attitude about a talent that was not there.

Therefore, though it's important to have big dreams and to have the power to go for it, in order for the power of positive thinking and positive acting to work for you, you must somewhere down the line give yourself a reality check. This doesn't mean that you relinquish your dreams; nor does it mean, as we discussed already, that you accept without question what others say about your abilities. It does, however, mean that if you are relying on one particular thing to happen in your life, one particular thing to bring you the success you want, you must obtain objective feedback to see if that dream is at all possible. Your self-assessment must somehow be grounded in reality. Winners do not set themselves up to suffer from unrealistic expectations. They know that expectations can be altered, helping them to find fulfillment rather than frustration in life.

Of course, this holds true in the business arena as well as the personal one. I encounter so many people who feel that they are executive material when they can't even do the job they currently have. They have a positive mental attitude about their potential advancement in their company, but it is not reality based.

Career counselors and life coaches will help you see your strengths and weaknesses. They can help you determine if you're shooting for the near impossible, the possible with hard work, or a possibility well within your reach. Remember, to have winning aim, winners position themselves realistically in relation to their target. Getting advice from an unbiased person with experience is invaluable. A good coach or counselor will help you ask yourself the questions that will enable you to assess if you have the talent, ability, and motivation to make it happen. They can also help you adjust your dreams, and are wonderful at providing you with the tools to ascertain whether you are thinking on the right track and setting yourself up to win.

So many people waste time trying to rebuild smashed, shattered, unachievable dreams. The key, however, is to build new and better dreams. Winners accept the fact that instead of trying to revive an old dream, putting their effort into building a better, brighter, and a newer dream is the ticket. Some keep hoping for the unrealistic to happen, and hope likes to sneak its way into our hearts. Hope is not enough, as Rick Page states in his latest book *Hope Is Not a Strategy*. Yes, we must beware of hope alone, because as Norman Cousins writes, "The human body experiences a powerful gravitational pull in the direction of hope." However, it is indeed new dreams—new dreams that are achievable—that will create great, new, realistic hope within you.

Next, you must make certain that with your wonderful positive attitude and action plan, you have not confused a sense of self-esteem with a sense of self-importance. Unfortunately, this confusion is happening all over—especially with child rearing. Have you noticed that the new trend in parenting is to make children feel special, wonderful, important, and often downright exceptional? Many parents are misguided. Instead of creating what is thought to be a sense of self-esteem, they are creating monsters with an attitude and demeanor of self-importance and self-superiority. John Rosemon raises a compelling question in a recent issue of *Hemispheres* magazine: "Why do kids who are made to feel so good tend to act so bad?"

Winners understand that self-confidence, self-worth, and self-positivism are essential, but you must make certain that in the self-pumping process, you don't become too narcissistic, too self-absorbed, or too self-indulgent. Winners know that it is critical to show respect for others. It is essential to be civilized. Socialization demands manners and esteem for others as well as oneself. I am certain that many popular sports and entertainment figures today would call themselves winners and truly scoff at my sentiments. Exceptions to the rule, of course, exist. However, we are in serious trouble as a society if we use those who have succeeded with deviant, crude, and uncaring behavior as our winning role models. Though it is important to have self-pride, being obnoxious about it will do nothing to encourage others to help you win (unless you have made it already and have the big bucks to dangle in front of their eyes). In any event, even under those circumstances, their loyalty will be in question.

Additionally, beware of the fine line between confidence and arrogance. Often people with a positive attitude take it one step too far and instead of having that can-do mentality, they develop a "can-do-anything-and-are-responsible-for-doing-everything" mentality. They start letting their ego rule.

There's a story told about Winston Churchill who was supposedly scheduled to address the entire United Kingdom in an hour. He hailed a cab in London's West End, and told the driver to jolly well step on it and drive as fast as he could to the BBC. The unaware cab driver told this harried pedestrian that he would have to find another cab. "Why the hell is that?" asked the annoyed prime minister. "Well" said the cabbie, "ordinarily it wouldn't be a problem, sir, but Mr. Churchill is broadcasting at six tonight and I want to get home in time to hear his always-important message to the people." Supposedly, Winston Churchill was so gratified by hearing this comment, that he pulled a pound note out of his wallet and handed it over to the cab driver. The cabbie took one look at the money he was handed, thought for a brief second, and then said, "Wait a minute, sir. Hop in. You must be a great tipper, and the hell with Mr. Churchill."

Remember, no one is without room for improvement and no one knows everything about anything. I have noticed that sometimes people's egos get out of balance and can really start to work against them. I have seen some people, who after attaining a certain level of success, after receiving a few awards or trophies, after reaching new goals and even perhaps creating new company profits, begin to think that they are really hot stuff. They start to gain a smugness. They change their attitude toward others. They treat colleagues in a condescending manner and may even act arrogantly toward management. Sometimes these superstars may even claim to be completely responsible for the company's turnaround or success.

To be a winner, you must never lose your humility. Loss of humility often leads to a loss of perspective—a loss of the real picture. That loss leads to a loss of focus, which eventually leads to the loss of your edge. So, as the great Tom Hopkins said, "Always enjoy the success experience you have earned, but never confuse confidence with arrogance."

In essence, never hope for more than you are willing to work for. Though you may not always get what you work for, you usually have to work for what you get. Remember that a positive mental attitude is a great and necessary winning foundation; however, it must be accompanied by work, realism, sensitivity to others, and positive, motivated action to really reap that winning prize.

Chapter

8

Winning Principle

*Winners Make Common Sense
Common Practice*

An African proverb states that there are forty kinds of lunacy but only one kind of common sense. The interesting thing to note, however, is that common sense is usually not commonplace. Nevertheless, winners realize the importance of exercising common sense, and work at making common sense common practice. Winners understand how performing the obvious, how engaging in the elementary, and how paying attention to the seemingly mundane can give them an enormous edge in life today.

Yes, doing the commonplace things in today's hectic and complex world sets you apart from the crowd, and tends to elevate others' opinion of you. You see, simply put, common sense has become downright uncommon. So winners shatter the stereotype. Yes, winners take a great deal of pride in doing what others do not do. Yes, winners do common-sense things uncommonly well.

Research reveals that today we supposedly spend about:

- 25.7 years of our lives in bed (and thanks to TV and videos, probably another 10 years watching others in bed).

- 7 years in the bathroom (some people spend a lot longer than that)

- 6 years eating (again, some spend a lot longer).

- 5 years waiting in line.

- 4 years cleaning our homes (they didn't poll me when they came up with this number; if cleanliness is next to Godliness, I guess I'm an atheist).

- 3 years attending unnecessary meetings.
- 2 years looking for things that we lost.
- 1 year waiting on hold.
- 8 months sitting at red lights.
- 6 months opening and throwing away junk mail.

And the list goes on.

Now perhaps you're thinking that those statistics don't accurately reflect your specific lifestyle. However, that makes no difference because there's still an important message revealed here: Life is collective and we do indeed measure out our lives in routine, little, often trivial and humdrum activities.

Yes, the mundane accounts for, and thereby impacts, a large part of our lives. In today's busy world, people often fail to realize that life is indeed made up of those little things. In fact, sooner or later, most of us learn that it's not the days in our lives that we remember; it's the moments. Winners know they can truly shine by making those moments, even if they seem ordinary, count.

Winners stand out from others by doing the ordinary in an extraordinary way. Both in the personal and professional arena, the little, common-sense things have a big effect on our lives. Yes, it is the obvious that's so often overlooked in favor of the more complex and more pressing issues. But, doing the little common-sense things well can make the biggest attention-getting difference.

In the bookstores, perhaps you have seen or even purchased the book *Don't Sweat the Small Stuff…and It's All*

Small Stuff. Well, I personally would have liked a more creative title—perhaps *Don't Sweat the Petty Stuff...and Don't Pet the Sweaty Stuff.* However, I've found that too many people who read this great book are getting the wrong idea. Of course, there are some people whose lives are dedicated to majoring in the minors, drowning in the drivel, and toiling with the trivial. Yes, there are many who worry over minutia to such a degree that it overtakes their lives and prevents them from moving forward. But the message "Don't sweat the small stuff" doesn't negate the importance of paying attention to the details in life. The message does not suggest ignoring the little, common-sense things that can indeed make a world of difference.

People focused totally on the big picture of fighting off the lions ignore those little pigeons that are nipping away at their toes and in the process causing tremendous damage. In a fast-paced world, we seem to think that the ordinary, everyday, commonplace things don't or won't matter. Winners know, however, that they are at the foundation of all that does indeed matter.

Winners know how often the obvious is overlooked. Winners know that the mark of an exceptional person is the ability to pay attention to both the big picture as well as the details. Yes, the common-sense concepts in life, the elements of life that more or less account for the "duh" factor, are becoming more and more difficult to find in daily practice.

Just last week, I had to go back to the office after dinner to start writing a speech. I turned on my computer, and nothing happened. To myself, I cursed, "Damn it, just when I'm in a crunch." So I took out my trusty Palm Pilot, pulled up the number for the emergency hot line, and made the call. After about 40 rings, a woman with an irritating voice answered. I explained my problem and the first words of advice out of her mouth were "Are you sure the computer is plugged in?" Boy, was I annoyed at that stupid, common-sense question. And you know what? I stayed annoyed even after I went ahead and reinserted the plug back into the outlet.

Too often, we operate on automatic pilot. Too often, we get SOS, stuck on stupid. Too often, we ignore the commonplace things to give our full attention to the more complex issues. Winners don't forget about one for the other. Winners do both. They are tuned in, at the same time, to both that large and small picture. In doing that they better market themselves and have more control over the total impact they make on others.

So, what are some of the common-sense and obvious details that winners pay close attention to and others largely ignore? Read on and rate yourself in terms of your dedication to the obvious. No matter how great you are in other aspects of your job, a low score in these five areas can diminish your winning ability and prevent you from moving on.

Winners Demonstrate and Practice Good Manners—Do You?

It has been said by many sociologists that today's society will take its place in history as being one of the most harried, frantic, competitive, violent, and unrefined times. It seems that civility, respect, manners, politeness, sensitivity to others, and social skills have nearly departed from the American scene. An interest in high IQ scores, advanced-placement classes, and being in the top percentile of one's class have become more important to parents than teaching children the art of civility, good breeding, and basic social graces. What are we in store for?

Yet, headhunters concur that in today's market place of human transactions, those social skills will indeed provide job candidates with a much better opportunity to differentiate themselves significantly from the crowd. Additionally, the vast majority of business gurus today agree that those skills are now, more than ever, a major factor in one's general success and specifically in attracting leadership opportunities.

I know a brilliant lawyer with a top Washington, D.C. law firm who serves as a perfect example of how lacking social skills can hold you back. Due to his amazing intelligence in his field and his Ivy League background, he was made a partner. However, he never received the accolades he wanted, never progressed to senior-partner status, never made as much money as other partners, never enjoyed a social relationship with anyone in his office, was kept out of the loop, and never commanded the respect he craved from others in his firm. Though brilliant in his field, he saw his success end there. He had no clue how to be affable, how to be cordial, how to project a sense of class and good breeding. The firm capitalized on his smarts to their advantage, but kept him down and out of the way.

Now, certainly there are some out there who have reached success without social skills, but in the business arena they are few and far between. The globalization of business has called for Americans to be more gracious, sensitive, and refined—and the rush is on to learn the way. Business executives are signing up for Manners 101, and classes teaching social graces are enjoying renewed interest and high enrollment. Leticia Baldrige's courses on manners have regained enormous popularity, and at many colleges today courses are offered in social etiquette.

It's interesting to note that the word "civilization" intimates that civility is present and accounted for. In these times, where so often we see that the milk of human kindness seems to have curdled, winners know that displaying basic manners, having social graces, and demonstrating a sensitivity for others' feelings must not go by the wayside. Winners share the philosophy that all people are worthy of respect until proven otherwise. Winners stand out from the crowd, and in many cases actually disarm others when they:

- Stand during introductions.
- Say please, thank you, and you're welcome.
- Look others in the eye when they speak.

- Look for ways to demonstrate acts of basic kindness.
- Hold doors for others.
- Display tact.

Just recently, after conducting a program, I was invited by one of my clients to his country club to join him and his staff for lunch. His sales manager and I entered the dining room at the same time. I have to admit that I was actually stunned when he pulled out my chair for me to be seated. I noticed also, when I excused myself before dessert to get to the airport in time for my flight, all the men at the table stood. I haven't experienced that in years. I can't tell you how that affected my entire perception of this company and how many times I've thought about those simple acts of good manners.

Recently, when a large prestigious association asked me to recommend a panelist for an upcoming national conference, the first person I thought of was that sales manager. I knew he was intelligent, but even more importantly, I knew he demonstrated good breeding. I knew he would not embarrass me.

Winners Know How to Market Their Face—Do You?

Winners know that of all the things they wear, the expression on their face is the most crucial. Yes, Armani, Pucci, Gucci, and Fendi will not mean a damn thing if the look on your face is sour, dour, or negative. Winners know that they have to market their face, and the basic way they do that is simply to start smiling more. Interestingly enough, people are actually smiling only one-third of the time that they think they are.

Now again, this seems like another no-brainer issue. However, in a world where the media has reinforced (or perhaps even created) the message that it's good to be bad and it's uncool to smile or show enthusiasm, convincing people to smile is not easy. Smiling, though, gains attention, sends out a favorable impression, projects success, and wins people over.

I heard one sociologist jokingly blame the sour appearances, grimness, and bad attitudes of teenage girls on the popularity of thong underwear. She claimed that if she had to walk around with a wedgie every day, she wouldn't be smiling either.

While the disaffected look may be "in" for the media, a smile is the ticket for the workplace. A smile is still considered an outward manifestation of success. Yes, if you smile, people tend to think you're happy and they also tend to think that one of the reasons you're happy is because you're doing well. Since people like to deal with people who do well, learn how to smile if you don't already do it naturally.

Winners know that smiling works to their advantage in many ways. I've noted that most winners have the ability to approach strangers and make them quick acquaintances even when the situation may be somewhat awkward. What helps them the most in this process is the expression on their face. Yes, a smile is a simple thing, but a huge asset. Success gravitates toward those people who appear to be successful. Winners know they must radiate success even if, at this particular time, they don't feel that way inside. The quickest and easiest way to do that is with a smile.

Winners Are Prompt—Are You?

Winners are prompt in returning phone calls and correspondence. Winners know that an easy way to separate themselves from others, to gain the attention of employers and customers, is simply to be prompt in this manner. In this climate of phone tag and voice mail, returning phone calls promptly, within the same morning or afternoon, will gain you positive attention and create a competent first impression with those you want to win over. Nothing frustrates a customer, client, or prospect more than an unreturned call. Responding promptly gives you an undeniable advantage in a world where we all tend to deal with people who are most accessible. Remember, if the competition can get back to customers and satisfy their need for products, services, information, or elaboration faster than you can, your business will suffer definitively.

Even though I mentioned earlier that routine phone calls should be held, to be answered during a specified hour of the day, your quick response to those important customers and clients will wow them!

Winners Have a Good Sense of Humor—Do You?

John Cleese, former *Monty Python* star and creator of the frenetic Basile Fawlty on the British comedy series *Fawlty Towers*, also produced a series of business-training tapes using his comedic flare. Cleese uses fun and laughter for entertainment as well as for business and educational purposes.

Cleese explained, "If I can get you to laugh with me, you like me better, which makes you more open to my ideas. And, if I can persuade you to laugh at a particular point that I make, by laughing at it you acknowledge it as true."

As a sales motivator, I know that laughter makes learning painless, and I also know that people who can agree on what is funny can usually agree on many other things as well. Humor in fact, enables you to get even a tough message across with better receptivity. When I'm conducting a program, I heed the words of film director Billy Wilder: "If you are going to tell people the truth, you better be funny or else they'll kill you."

Winners like humor. They like to laugh and project a happy persona. Winners know that when there is laughter in the air, people:

- Take more risks.

- Consider more options.

- Feel more empowered.

- Act more invigorated.
- Experience a greater sense of hope.
- Pay better attention.
- Consider themselves more capable.
- Put things in better perspective.
- Work more like a team.
- Level the playing field.
- Perform better.

Humor in the workplace can actually increase productivity! Robert Half International conducted a survey of one hundred vice presidents of major corporations. The study revealed that 84 percent of these executives thought that employees with a sense of humor performed better on the job than those with little or no sense of humor. Additionally, thanks to the work and philosophy of Dr. Norman Cousins, laughter has been known for years to strengthen the immune system. Yes, a good laugh can indeed:

- Increase your blood circulation.
- Raise your heart rate.
- Work your abdominal muscles.
- Evacuate some of the stale air from your lungs.
- Lower the levels of the stress hormone, cortisol.

It seems clear that Bobby McFerrin's hit song "Don't Worry, Be Happy" carries a medical endorsement. A study

reported in the *Mayo Clinic Proceedings* looked at mea-
surements of optimism and pessimism as a risk fact for
death. The researchers looked at 839 patients over a 30-year
period. In general, the study concluded that happy people
live longer than people who are not happy. So, though
laughter can be a sign of nervousness, or even fear, it is most
associated with happiness. Laughter and happiness can
contribute to your physical and fiscal health. It is true that
"those who laugh, last." I even heard once that if you're inclined to laugh, and suppress it, restrain it, harbor it, or keep
it in, it will push down and spread to your hips. That scared
the hell out of me because I'm at a time in my life when my
fear of heights has been replaced by a fear of widths.

I repeatedly advise managers all over this country that
if they want to create a productive team that really works
together in harmony, they must blend business with a
good deal of pleasure. People like to do business with
those who show that they like doing business. Margaret
Thatcher had it right when she said, "There is profit
in other peoples pleasure." (Or was it Heidi Fleiss who
said that?)

Now, having a sense of humor doesn't mean that you
have to be funny. (By the way, funny people do not necessarily say funny things. They say things funny.) It means
that you have to appreciate humor in others. Also, having
a fun attitude doesn't mean that you don't take your work
seriously. Winners know that taking your work seriously is
an essential element of success. However, taking yourself

seriously is an element of disaster. If you can't laugh at yourself, you leave that task for someone else to carry out—and that is downright frightening.

It has been said that man is actually the only animal that can laugh. By the way, we are also the only animal that takes back our young once they've left the nest, but that's another story. The point is, take advantage of that exclusive laughing ability.

Steve Lundin, along with John Christensen and Harry Paul, wrote *Fish*, which delves into how workers at the Pike Fish Market in Seattle stay motivated with laughter, a sense of humor, and a fun work environment. The basic message is that no matter what you do, on-the-job drudgery is avoidable. They have found that the fun-work philosophy, which they call "Fish," is based on the premise that on-the-job fun increases workforce commitment as well as creativity. The book describes several workplaces that have been fun-injected. Many were high-stress environments and many were companies who paid their employees modestly. In each instance, when fun was in the air and when unconventional behavior was celebrated, performance accelerated.

I recently spoke with J. Walker Smith from the Yankelovich Partners, an outstanding research group. Among other issues, a recent Yankelovich study highlighted the fact that though we live in extraordinary times, most people are still bored. The explanation is that just as cocaine users develop a tolerance to the drug and require bigger and bigger doses to keep getting the same high, we too, as a society, have developed an amazing tolerance to astonishing and remarkable events. Though of course there are many issues that contribute to this boredom, Yankelovich concludes that a large part of the problem is that, "We are a high-input society...living amidst a babble of signals. We must listen to a great deal of chatter to hear the one bit of information we really want."

The study goes on to say that what cuts through to the consumer, what helps them overcome boredom, what proves to clear out the chatter and the clutter, and gain their attention is—you guessed it—humor. Seventy-two percent of the 100 best commercials of all time used humor to reach their targeted audience. Humor and laughter help us cope with the turbulent times in which we live; and they also provide many benefits in the personal and business arenas.

Winners Copy Success—Do You?

This is not to say that winners are not inventive, creative, and original. Nor is this to suggest that I recommend emulation over innovation. However, winners observe, study, and copy other winners and their approach to success. Yes, there are universals among winners and if you want to be a winner, too, you can get a jump-start by replicating what other winners have done. You don't have to reinvent the proverbial wheel. Emulating others' successes is a simple concept but, believe it or not, is rarely done. Look at the French, for example; they continue to build Peugeots.

Peugeots don't go. Why don't they just look at the Japanese? The Japanese build cars that go. They build cars that people buy. The Japanese make a good deal of money selling their wonderful cars. Just copy the concept.

Personally, I had a great deal of copying experience in math classes when growing up. I recall those algebra test instructions "Show how you arrived at your answers on a separate sheet of paper." When following those instructions, I always had to draw a picture of myself copying off the guy next to me! That didn't work too well. In the business arena, the work of others can serve as rough templates for our own work. Winners do the obvious: They look, watch, listen and imitate. It is the highest form of flattery.

Winners know that little things actually make a huge difference in one's success path. In light of this, I'm reminded of the Butterfly Effect, a term which came about as the result of work done by Edward Lorenz, a meteorologist from MIT. Basically, Lorenz's work related to how more complicated, easily changeable and adaptive systems like weather patterns can be compellingly affected by very small and unlikely influences.

However, when we open our eyes, we can see that small and unlikely influences profoundly affect other complicated, easily changeable and adaptive systems as well: The political scene, the stock market, a company's culture, your personal mood, and even your own success.

The culture of a corporation is comprised of many things, but principally by what I call its personality. Executives today must insist on respect for all, good manners, visibly happy dispositions, promptness in response, and a fun attitude. Everyone today must understand how these details, how making these small changes, can greatly influence your big-life picture. Edmund Burke said, "Nobody makes a greater mistake than he who did nothing because he could only do a little." Winners know that no one makes a greater mistake than the person who did nothing because they thought it would not be noticed.

Yes, little changes make big difference. Paul Friedman, editor of the *Pryor Report*, said that his research proved that top managers at most large companies earn up to 10 times more than frontline employees. He wondered why they were rewarded so much better. Friedman questioned: Do they work 10 times harder? Do they work 10 times longer? Do they have 10 times the ability? The answer, say Jonathan and Susan Clark, lies in what is called the Law of the Slight Edge. This law simply reiterates what I emphasized earlier: Small changes over time make big differences. Just being slightly better, having slightly better methods of training or planning, having slightly better policies, or making slightly wiser decisions can work wonders. One crucial decision, which might seem trivial, is **Do the obvious.**

Donald Trump said, "As long as I'm thinking, I'm going to think big." Though I certainly encourage that, I also know that to get really big, you have to think small as well. I love ANA Airlines slogan: "Attention to details isn't written in our training manuals, it's in our DNA." How lucky!

Winning Principle

Winners Know That the Nature of Any
Relationship Is Based on Communication

In a world that is relationship-oriented, winners know the important role that communication can play in fostering, maintaining, strengthening, or destroying a relationship. Whether the relationship is between employer and employee, one business associate and another, mother and daughter, father and son, brother and sister, or husband and wife is of no consequence. The fact of the matter is, if you can talk to one another easily, you most likely have a good relationship with that person, and if you can't communicate easily, you don't. This is not an oversimplification of a concept. This is a bottom line reality and one that's too easily glossed over when trying to connect with others.

Yes, winners understand the correlation between easy communication and positive relationships. Winners know that the preferences people have in terms of who they choose to deal with, who they want to associate with, and who they seem to gravitate toward, are heavily influenced by the perceived similarity or differences in the communication style and process used by that other person.

This doesn't mean that you have to imitate the communication patterns of others you wish to impact or win over. However, it does mean that being more *flexible* in your communication approach, being aware of damaging communication pitfalls, and knowing what communication styles most people are attracted to will help you to gain more of a winning relationship edge with others you are trying to impress, influence, or just add to your business and personal circle.

Since we live in global times, the concept of communicating effectively with others can seem overwhelming, as each culture has its own communication nuances. However, being able to curse in five languages does not make you a multicultural communicator.

Understanding the foundation that communication plays in forming relationships is not as easy as one might think. For example, getting down to business quickly with a new client may be part of your own company's corporate culture; however, with an Asian client, that tactic will destroy a potential relationship faster than a speeding bullet. Casual banter, for most Asian businesspeople, is as much a part of the transaction as the actual deal, and shooting the breeze is an important prelude to conducting business and forming strong business associations.

Communication differences can result in laughable, as well as frightening, experiences. While sitting in a taxi in Seoul, Korea I could hardly believe my eyes while reading a sign attached to the back of the drivers seat that stated, "If you have experienced painful intercourse in this car, please report it to this taxi company immediately." I later realized that in Korea the word "intercourse" is used primarily to mean "conversation" and the word "painful" translates as "distressful."

Though the preceding example is quite understandable in terms of misinterpretation, communication challenges don't just happen while dealing with people from other countries. No, we can have communication mishaps that are equally or even more disastrous with those a lot closer to home, and with those of a similar back-ground.

Recently I was returning from a trip to Vancouver, British Columbia, and it was rather late at night. The plane was only half-full, but I still noticed the normal cadre of business suits using their laptops, catching some Zs, or watching the latest Gwyneth Paltrow movie.

An interesting-looking gentleman sitting alone caught my eye. He appeared to be about 75, had deep craggy lines in his chiseled face, was dressed in neat jeans with a string tie, wasn't watching the movie either, but was reading a novel by Robert Parker, a master at writing dialogue and one of my favorite authors.

I was bored and curious, so I went up to him and started talking about the book. After awhile, I discovered that though he now lived in Montana, during the same two-year period we lived about eight blocks from each other in Maplewood, New Jersey. As our conversation progressed, I also learned that he was currently a ranch hand and loved what he did.

Now if "ranching" were the final question on *Jeopardy*, I would bet zero. In other words, this is one of those topics that I know absolutely nothing about. But, he spoke English, I spoke English, and what a wonderful opportunity this was to learn a little about the subject.

We bantered back and forth a bit and then I asked him if he worked on a big ranch. He responded that actually his ranch was quite small. I pressed on to learn what exactly his job entailed. He answered that his primary responsibility involved getting the bull out of his corral every morning to join the cows in their corral so they could mate.

"On a small ranch, shouldn't the owner, himself be doing that?" I asked. Then, looking at me rather quizzically, he hesitantly replied, "No, it has to be a bull." It was also at this point that he pressed the flight attendant button and started watching the movie with incredible interest.

Deborah Tannen, author of *You Just Don't Understand*, and John Grey, author of the *Men Are From Mars Women Are From Venus* book series, achieved worldwide notoriety and popularity discussing communication differences between men and women. But that is just the edge of the abyss.

Yes, communicating with clarity—communicating for mutual understanding, communicating so it has positive impact, communicating with ease—is not a simple task. However, winners understand how important those concepts are and how positive communication can powerfully affect relationships. Therefore, they work with an understanding of these five general, yet critical, communication concepts. Let's take a look at them before moving on to some specific winning communication tactics.

Critical, Communication Concepts

Test yourself to see how many of these you are currently aware of:

1. *One of the greatest obstacles in communication is the illusion that it transpired the way you intended it.* The

rancher story demonstrates this. Checking for clarity and understanding must never be assumed when the dialogue is important. Winners are always saying phrases like, "Do I understand you to mean?," "Are you telling me that…?," "Let me rephrase this to make certain we're on the same page," "Did I understand you to mean what I thought I heard you say?"

2. *You cannot not communicate.* Yes, I know that two negatives make a positive. However, it's important to understand that if you have ever labeled someone as uncommunicative, you were wrong. They were communicating something. They were communicating the fact that they didn't wish to communicate with you. People are always sending out communiqués, whether intentional or not—if not by words or lack of words then by facial expressions or body language.

3. *Words have power, but other elements of speech have power as well.* Consider your:

Tone: Does your voice have inflection? Does it radiate enthusiasm? Do you sound boring? Dylan Thomas was known for saying, "Someone is boring me, and I think it is me."

Pace: Do you speak so slowly or so quickly that you lose others? Given the choice as to whether to speak on the slow side or the fast side, winners (as most great leaders) usually speak more quickly. Today, especially, people lose patience with others who speak too slowly.

Believe it or not, the average person can absorb about 760 words per minute.

Pitch: Lower sounds are easier to listen to. Higher ones project less self-assurance and are often grating, causing others to tune out. Women usually have longer and thinner vocal chords than men thus making their voices higher. Of all the things that could have been naturally longer and thinner with women, what a waste that we're talking about vocal chords here.

Projection: Projection is not about loudness but about the power of your voice, its degree of richness and fullness, its ability to carry and resonate.

Pauses: Silence can be very powerful. The best communicators use silence for emphasis as well as for control. An ardent admirer once asked Arthur Rubinstein how he handled the notes so well. The famous pianist responded that he handled the notes no better than many others, but he handled the pauses in a superior way.

Physical posture: This refers to your stance and carriage. Albert Mehrabian, in his teachings and research at UCLA, said that communication impact comes from three things: your words, your voice, and your body language. To be specific, he felt that when you are in an influencing arena, 7 percent of your power will come from your words, or what you actually say. Thirty-eight percent will come from your voice, or how you say what you say, but 55 percent will come from your body language, or how you look when you say what you say. Yes, he proved that communication involved much more than words alone—and he knew what he was talking about.

Think about the fact that we use negative body language descriptions to describe poor performance. "He's in a slump. She's a slouch. They're a drag." Instead of spending time trying to interpret others' body language, spend more time improving your own. Good posture is still positively correlated with class and success; and standing tall even brings more oxygen to the brain to help you think more clearly.

4. *The environment greatly affects the communication process.* Let's say that you have an idea that you want to bounce off your boss for approval. When you enter his office, you notice that his desktop is completely covered with paperwork, his potted palm is on its last leg, his trash can is full, a rotten banana peel sits on top of his credenza, and his desk blotter is covered with coffee rings. If that's the case, the chances that your boss will be receptive to your ideas and give you approval just diminished significantly. Environments do affect receptivity.

However, if, upon entering your boss's office, you note that a vase filled with fresh flowers has been placed on his credenza, the cleaning crew is now using a spray scent that is amazingly similar to Halston, the widows have obviously just been washed, the carpeting has been recently vacuumed, and the desk is relatively neat, your request for time, attention, and idea approval, has just significantly and dramatically increased.

The effect the environment has in terms of communication can be seen on the home front as well. If my husband wants to make up after a disagreement and tries to do so while I am leaning over the kitchen sink with a Brillo pad in my hands, he can hang it up. However, if he were to take me out to a little Italian bistro with soft lighting, soothing music, and luscious aromas (the bouquet of a nice cabernet can also help), you would be amazed at how quickly I forgive him.

Yes, the environment can positively or adversely affect the communication attempt. So, especially when seeking positive feedback from others, make certain that you never underestimate the importance of a pleasant environment.

5. *The greater the need to communicate, the more challenging it becomes.* Anyone who has ever had to fire a business associate who was also a friend can vouch for this. The awkwardness of the situation, the delicacy it demands, the importance of saying the right words, makes this entire task a very difficult one to handle. Even on a personal note, one can relate to the difficulty in finding the right words when the right words are so important. How many of us have struggled with finding the right sentiments to express to a dear friend who just lost a spouse or a parent?

Therefore, realize that when the message is delicate, or especially critical, it has no reflection on your ability to communicate if you take some up front time to think it through. Being a good communicator has little to do with being improvisational.

Some winners seem to know the importance of these guidelines and use them to be a more effective communicator innately. Others just seem to learn quickly from experience.

Winning Communication Tactics

Now, let's move on to some of those specific talk tactics that foster communication give and take. Do as winners do, and use them to help you potentially launch the relationship of a lifetime.

Talk simply. Jack Welch, when CEO of General Electric said, "You can't believe how hard it is for people to be simple, how much they fear being simple. They worry that if they're simple, people will think they're simple-minded. In reality, of course, it's just the reverse. Clear, tough-minded people are the most simple." Only amateurs feel the need to use fancy jargon to try to impress others. Winners demonstrate clear thinking by delivering their messages in a way that most people can easily understand. Denzel Washington in the movie *Philadelphia* said, "Talk to me like I'm three."

His message would be a test that most winners could easily pass. When communicating, I have found that genius is the ability to trim down the complicated to the straightforward.

Get to the point: Unfortunately in most English classes today, they don't teach the art of summarizing. Yet, this is a critical communication skill in a world where people listen in sets of six- to eight-second sound bytes and where Attention Deficit Disorder has become the diagnosis du jour. Remember, people today are junkies for anything fast, and that not only goes for their food preferences.

It's an old adage that art reflects life, and since music is an art form, one can look at its evolution in terms of popularity and draw many life conclusions.

At one time, songs of a more esoteric nature were popular; symbolism and metaphors were used: "I'd Rather Be a Hammer Than A Nail," "Someone Left the Cake out in the Rain." Today, our fast lives don't allow us the time to interpret, and, boy oh boy, doesn't music reflect that. Some say that country western music, the most popular music in America today, gained its status because the messages are so to the point. No interpretation time required here. Just the titles alone spell it all out fast— "You Can Take This Job and Shove It," " You're the Reason Our Kids Are Ugly," "If Your Phone Doesn't Ring, You Know It's

Me," "I Still Miss You Baby but My Aim's Getting Better," and, of course, Steven Bishop's, "I'm So Miserable without You It's Almost Like Having You Here."

Practice the art of summarization with a simple story. Eventually move on to more involved scenarios, but do practice. You will be amazed how quickly you'll start to eliminate the ramble, get to the point, keep others' attention better, and have much more impact.

Make sure that you are a positive speaker and that you are not inadvertently sending out negative messages. Dr. J. Mitchell Perry said that negative talk creeps into our language as we mature. In children, positivism reigns: Ask a child how they enjoyed their trip to Disney world and you will hear comments like, "It was awesome, and a lot of fun" or "It was cool." Ask a parent the same question and the response will most likely be something like "Not nearly as rough as I though it would be" or "Not too bad."

Dr. Perry said that in microcosm this little example demonstrates the subtle changes that overtake people's language as they transition from the more inherent optimism of childhood to the more pessimistic outlook of adulthood.

The rub is that what you say, what you think, and how you feel are all connected. Yes, thinking, feeling, and communicating all impact each other and not necessarily in any order. Picture a triangle with the word "think" on one angle, "feel" on another, and "say" on the third. Now it doesn't matter what angle you start with, one element will

affect the other two. In other words, how you *think* will affect what you say and how you feel. How *feel* will affect
what you say and how you think. What you *say* will affect
how you think and how you feel.

If you can just change one of these three elements
(thinking, feeling, or saying), you can indeed change your
life. Changing what you **say** is by far the easiest thing to
tackle. Doing so will not only affect how you think and
how you feel, but it will change the way others perceive
you and are influenced by you as well. By simply changing
your language to be more positive and optimistic, you can
improve your personal attitude and have a significantly
better impact on everyone you meet. Yes, if you change
your language, you can change your life. So start making
these little changes now:

- Avoid the phrase "don't forget" and replace it with
  the word "remember."

It has been proven that the mind has a real problem
with do's and don'ts in that it often ignores or confuses
them. Therefore, "Don't forget that report is due at 4:00 can
actually translate as, "Forget that report is due at 4 o'clock."
You will project the image of a more positive person and
have much better luck using the word "remember" instead.
By the way, "don't forget" is somewhat of a subtle put down,
as if you were intimating they were going to forget.

- Use the term "I will" instead of "I won't." It's common for people to say something like "I won't look
  at that report until it's been proofed." Instead,

strengthen your can-do image by saying "I will look at that report as soon as it's proofed." Talk about what you will do, as opposed to what you won't do.

- Change your wording to be more optimistic and positive. For example:

Instead of:	Say:
I can't argue with that.	I'm inclined to agree with that.
I don't have a problem with that.	I'll go with that.
I hope you don't mess up	I anticipate you doing very well.
Don't let me get in your way.	I'll get out of your way.
Let's not get into that now.	Let's talk about that later.
I'm not worried.	I'm confident.
Why can't you?	How about?
I should have.	Starting from now on I will.

Negative speech patterns are often used to avoid responsibility as well as to deflect enthusiasm, which some out-of-touch people feel is uncool. The fact of the matter is that just by executing these little communication changes in your life, you will feel differently, others will view you differently, you can more easily eliminate some of the barriers of resistance, and you will discover that people are much more cooperative. I think that sometimes our tongue gets in the way of our eyeteeth and we just can't see the impact of what we are saying.

Chapter

10

Winning Principle

*Winners Know That Listening Is
the Most Important Thing They
Can Do in Any Relationship*

Sitting next to a woman at a leadership consortium recently, I learned that she was a well-known psychotherapist. After awhile, we began talking about the challenges we face personally as well as in our careers. I asked her how she could possibly be such a positive person after spending hours upon hours every day having people tell her about their trials, tribulations, anxieties, doubts, disappointments, compulsions, disorders, paranoia, and neurosis. "Easy," she answered, " I just don't listen." I squeaked out a little nervous laugh, assuming that this was a feeble attempt at humor. At least I hope it was.

It's apparent, however, that whether it involves paying big bucks to have a professional ostensibly listen to your problems or whether it involves entering a listening booth at a mall in California, where for a more modest fee, someone, anyone, just gives you their quiet attention, listening has evolved into a rare and hard-to-find human quality. I know it's rare because it made the news when a group of people in Los Angeles held up signs that read, "Talk to us. We'll listen" and people lined up. Yes, a good listener is a real find, and demonstrating or developing that rare listening ability can be a huge asset in the business arena as well as on the personal front.

Being a good listener can reap many rewards, and winners know that once a relationship has been formed, demonstrating those important listening skills will not only keep it going but also keep it strong and solid. In fact, winners know that **listening is the single most important thing they can do in any relationship they have.**

The irony is that, though listeners are hard to find, most people will agree that talkers are everywhere. Perhaps the complexity of our world gives people more to say. Possibly there are just so many more people who want to test their right to free expression. Conceivably it's because "speak when spoken to" has been replaced by "if you don't ask, you don't get." Perhaps it's because we live with more frustration, and talking about it helps us to vent. Or maybe in our high-input society, listening to learn that one bit of relevant information amidst all the babble has become too exhausting a task. Whatever the reason may be, it does, however, seem almost ludicrous that in a society where so many sophisticated and state-of-the-art listening devices exist, we have such a limited supply of good and willing listeners.

But the fact of the matter is that talk is indeed cheap— and I'm certain that it has to do with the simple law of supply and demand.

People today seem to have a lot to say and they want to be heard. Unfortunately, most don't understand that being heard does not necessarily mean they are actually being listened to. Remember, we hear with our ears, but we listen with our minds. Engaging that mind power, turning on that portion of one's brain that gives a damn, is what real listening is all about.

Seeing that in action or experiencing it is rather uncommon in a world where more people seem intent on getting their two cents in rather than engaging in the harder work that real listening involves.

Real listening, listening with the purpose of gaining insight and understanding, listening with the purpose of showing concern and interest, is called *active* listening as opposed to *passive* listening. Passive listening, however, does occur when perhaps we listen to background music or a radio talk show more for the company value rather than for the message.

However, when you engage in active listening you are involved in both the message and the messenger. When you actively listen, you become impacted by both in a significant way. When you actively listen, you process the information gleaned to later use or refer to in some manner. Perhaps you will use what was learned to better understand the speaker's point of view. Perhaps you will use what was learned to provide relevant feedback; perhaps you will use what was learned to simply show the speaker that you have fine-tuned listening skills.

Of course, to be an active listener, you must be more than attentive. You must have Discipline, Interest, a Sincere desire to understand, and Concentration: These are called the DISC elements of listening. And, trust me, your DISC is not too full to absorb more. Yes, keen, active, and astute listening requires:

Discipline: Yes, you must have the control to allow others to speak and to squelch the urge to jump in and start talking.

Interest: You must show concern for the speaker and demonstrate a visible interest in being in their presence and grasping their message.

Sincere desire to understand: You must demonstrate your intention to actually process and comprehend the message the speaker wishes to convey. As Dr. Stephen Covey says in *The Seven Habits of Highly Effective People*, it's essential to understand before attempting to be understood.

Concentration: You must have the power to resist being sidetracked by extraneous movement, other nearby conversations, or your own thoughts. In business today, the expression "**squint your ears**" refers to zeroing in on what is being said above all else at the moment.

These four elements are critical traits that all great active listeners have, and that winners nurture or acquire.

It has been said that perhaps history wouldn't have to repeat itself if people were listening better. And, it has not just been historians who have warned that we are not listening as carefully as we should to what experience teaches.

Larry King recently restated this often ignored fact: "The only time I learn is when I'm listening." However, besides the most obvious aspect of listening, which is indeed to learn, winners know that no one ever listened themselves out of a job. Listening enhances both our professional and personal lives in a world where gathering nuances to gain the competitive advantage is profitable, setting oneself apart is essential, and attracting others to you and your cause is critical.

Psychiatrist Karl Menninger called listening a creative force, as well as a magnetic one. (The other evening, my husband joked that I must be a magnetic force because everything I was wearing was charged). Menninger said that the people who listen to us are the ones we move toward. He said that we want to sit in their radius, and that when we are listened to, it creates us. When one listens to us, it makes us unfold as well as expand and elaborate.

Yes, active listeners get more out of the person speaking to them. Their demonstrative listening ability not only encourages the speaker to offer more, but it also creates a bond, a feeling of shared history with the listening party.

Winners have learned that, for the most part, listening is not the opposite of talking. No, generally speaking, the opposite of talking is waiting—waiting for the other person to stop talking so you can get your turn to jump in and speak what's on your mind. In fact, it's been said that when others are talking, most people are only focused on framing what their next response will be. Maybe it's time for Toastmaster's International to look at the flip side and teach people to listen, instead of to talk.

Many early childhood specialists feel that children today need a good listening to, not a good talking to. Showing others that you are willing to take the time to hear what they have to say is not only the highest form of flattery but translates as a real sign of caring.

In the business arena, employees are beginning to interpret listening as a form of praise and during the interview process; employers are more and more interested in determining one's listening skills often over and above one's speaking skills. I have heard many of my clients tell me that they have determined that it is far easier to teach someone to be an effective speaker than it is to teach someone to be an active and effective listener.

Think about your listening skills. Make certain that you are not sabotaging your ability to be an active listener from the very start. Do you frequently find yourself falling into anyone of these categories below? How often do you enter into conversations with others in one of these modes?

The mind reader: You're thinking, "Been there, done that" or "I've heard it already and I know what they are going to say before they even say it."

The rehearser: You feel that your response will be so important that you couldn't possibly give anyone else your attention; instead you have to formulate and mentally practice what you'll be saying next.

The analyst: You're intent on ciphering the hidden meanings and the unsaid messages the speaker is giving. You frequently say to yourself, "Hmm, I wonder what he really means by that. Let me try to interpret this message."

The selector: You find yourself frequently justifying inattention by thinking, "I'm not going to listen to all this stuff. I'm savvy enough to just tune in when the subject sounds important and relevant to me personally."

The rusher: You're frequently impatient with others. "Yada, yada, yada, come on, come on already, get to the point."

The relater: From the start, you assess the situation and feel, "They are so me. I can clearly identify with their feelings here. I know exactly the point they're making." No matter what they say, you feel that it will coincide with what you would say.

The fighter: You are willing to sit and pretend to listen, but you already know that this person is totally wrong from the start. You don't even give her a chance to present her viewpoint and logic. It's déjà-moo—you've heard this bull before.

If you find yourself frequently in one or more of the preceding modes, you have some work to do on that important winning trait—listening. Before you enter into any corrective behavior, consider the following points:

1. *Remember that listening really means hearing others.* It does not count if, after the first few sentences, you start giving advice or adding your own personal opinion or feedback. When you do that, you block out the immediate thoughts of the speaker and can also miss the entire message.

2. *Don't necessarily feel that when someone wants you to listen, they also want your solutions and feedback.* Many people find that hearing themselves talk it out to an interested party provides them with the first and best means to problem-solve on their own. Often what people need when they engage you in conversation is an interested and concerned ear. They're not necessarily looking for a fixer or a solutionist.

When you can listen without interjecting your thoughts, it becomes almost a spiritual experience for the talker. It has been said that prayer works for so many because the Lord is mute and no advice is offered. What is offered instead is just the trust that you will work it all out for yourself.

3. *Listening is actually a motivator.* When others realize that you are truly attentive and interested in what is on their mind, they often feel compelled to follow through with their verbalized intentions. Remember, as I said earlier, that one of the best ways to tackle a project you've been postponing is to start telling others that you're now committed and ready to get to it.

4. *Listening is a time saver.* Yes, if you engage in active listening, you'll save a great deal of time. Though repetition may in fact be the mother of learning, getting that message the first time it's sent out puts you ahead of the game.

5. *Though many people, especially after years of schooling, have become quite adept at faking the listening process, most people today can tell whether your interest in listening to them is genuine or not.* How many of you have been in situations where another person asks you a question, and as you begin answering it, you note their eyes leave you and start scanning the room? What do you do? Well, unless you're so self-absorbed that you can't see what's happening, you stop talking right on the spot. You also will tend to remember that incident. Yes, once that slight happens to you, your

opinion of that room-gazer quickly and irreparably goes downhill.

6. *It's been said that if you listen more than you speak, you will usually be perceived as more intelligent than you really are.* If you've ever seen the movie *Being There* with Peter Sellers and Shirley McLaine, you'll recall the incredible power that Sellers' character, Chauncy Gardner, had from doing very little talking and instead engaging in a great deal of listening.

Yes, listening is a critical component of effective communication. I have joked that my husband and I have no problem communicating. You see, he was a communication major in college and I majored in theater arts. So, our system for a long relationship is simple. Because of his training, he communicates very well, and because of my training, I *act* like I am listening very well.

It is not enough today to just act like your listening; you actually have to **show** it. Here are some less obvious but critical ways you can show others that you are an astute and active listener.

- *Always let others finish their sentences.* Interrupters do more to demonstrate their lack of patience than their understanding and interest.

- *Even if you feel as if you can make assumptions, fight the urge.* You may miss a great deal of important information by prematurely jumping to conclusions.

- *From time to time, take notes as others talk.* This not only will serve as a reminder to you regarding pertinent points made, but it always serves to make the speaker feel important. And, people like people who make them feel important.

- *Don't feel the need to fill in the pauses.* Pauses, as I mentioned earlier, can be used for punctuation and drama. There's a space between stimulus and response. Let it stay there. In fact, often when listening to others, you will note that a very important point is made—either just prior to or right after that pause was taken.

- *Make eye contact.* This isn't as easy as you think. If nothing else, television programming has proven that we would almost rather look at anything else than each other. On the other hand, beware of course, of getting into a staring mode. Glance at your notes occasionally, and when looking at the speaker, instead of looking directly into both eyes, look at one eye, then the other. It keeps the effect of eye contact going without the potential feeling of intimidation, discomfort, or threat.

- *Offer nonverbal encouragement through an interested facial expression and appropriate head nodding.*

- *Physically lean in toward the speaker.* Unfortunately, most people tend to lean away or lean back when another is speaking. The distance you put between yourself and another unconsciously says a lot about your interest level.

- *Refrain from clicking your pen, strumming your fingers, or tapping your foot when others are speaking.* Not only do these acts show impatience, but they also serve as a distraction to the speaker as well as to you, the listener.

- *When the time is right, always take a moment to summarize what's been covered.* This promotes clarity as well as progress.

- *Listen for the emotion being expressed while the words are being said.*

- *From time to time, without interrupting, repeat something that the speaker said.* This is a quick way to demonstrate your listening ability and interest.

- *Don't be afraid to ask clarifying questions when appropriate.*

- *If you know in advance that listening to this particular person tends to bring out the bear within, program yourself to engage in what is called a positive-index listening exercise.* In other words, attend the session or meeting with the commitment to not only listen all the way through, but to especially note anything positive or complementary that might be said. Look for harmony and be aware when something is said that coincides with your way of thinking.

My friend and mentor the late Jim Mills, author of *Action Selling,* used the term *productive listening* when he would teach. To sum it up, he would say that active listeners not only get the information they are seeking, but also through their body language, reflect a genuine sense of concern and an attitude that demonstrates indisputable interest and a total commitment to the speaker at this moment in time.

Being able to listen in this manner encourages the speaker to expand, elaborate, and perhaps give you important details that you might have had to learn on your own. Yes, as a bonus, a good listener often gets information others would not be privy to.

Perhaps even more importantly, it must be understood that sincere listening can enhance a relationship and cement a bond that is difficult to duplicate through any other venue.

My advice is to do what winners do. When trying to make a positive impression, listen, get the facts, assess the situation, and realize that in the process you are building an unconscious affinity with the speaker. Listen like a lover. Hang on to every word even if you've heard the story 10 times before, laugh at the jokes, and show genuine interest in the message as well as the messenger. Fine-tuned listening skills almost always guarantees a unique position in that winners circle.

Chapter

11

Winning Principle

Winners Are Energized by Change,
Not Traumatized by It

Man's resistance to change has been a theme throughout history. Writers from Shakespeare to Anton Chekhov to Shirley Jackson have written powerful stories about how people fight change. Change has been defined, in modern times, as the ability to give up the familiar—yet the familiar is hard to give up.

Charles Darwin, however, said that the species that survives will not necessarily be the smartest or the strongest, but it will be the species that is most adaptable to change. Winners know that change is going to happen with them or without them. They know that change is here to stay, that it's the only constant, and that we ain't seen nothing yet. Winners know that change is inevitable, (unless of course you're using a vending machine). Winners also know that if you can't get out of it, you had best get into it— and change is one of those things no one can escape from.

Change is ubiquitous. Remember when hardware referred to nails, hammers, hinges, and the like? Remember when a hot tub was a stolen bathtub, when a floppy disc meant you had a bad back, when a cursor was a person who used bad language, when logging on meant adding wood to the fire, and when a hard drive referred to a three-hour car trip with the kids fighting in the backseat?

Change. You can run, but you won't be able to hide. Change is going to find you one way or the other. We live in a time of unparalleled change: New ideas, new morality,

new technology, new perspectives, new concepts. We live
in a world with:

Spirit guides
Ghost busters
Centering groups
Pet psychics
Bioenergetics
Primal therapy
Guided imagery
Yoga-holics
Magnetic healing
Channeling
Rolfing
Aroma rehabilitation
Grounding
Holographic memory resolution
Rebirthing
Homeschooling
Self-parenting
Qigong
Inversion swings
Snoring clinics
Flowers essences
Harmonic brain-wave synergy
Psycho-calisthenics
Wrestle-mania
Hot coal jogging

Nerve stimulation
Kelp and spinach rubdowns
Nude volleyball teams
And . . .
White-wine hot-tub therapy (which sounds like a wonderful idea to me)

Along with massive changes, complexity has entered the picture. Have you noticed that you can't even have a leisurely chat on the phone anymore, while sipping a cup of coffee and eating a bagel, without some idiot behind you honking his horn.

Change was always recognized as an issue in man's evolution, but it's the speed of change now that boggles the mind. (I still remember when people were aghast that learning doubled every seven years.) Did you know that there has been more information produced in the last 30 years than during the previous 5,000? Yes, the speed of change today makes life increasingly confusing. Not only is it difficult to keep up with the new; it's also hard to understand how so much of it came to be. For example, they now sell lemon juice with artificial flavoring, but they sell lemon floor polish with real lemon juice. Maybe I'll a put a little Mop and Glo in my next cup of tea.

When I was growing up, I ate lard from a tub and thought I'd live forever. Now we use I Can't Believe It's Not Butter spray. Well, I believe it is not butter—I believe it's WD40.

Technology, though I try to stay current with all the changes, confuses me even more. The cars we drive have more computer power than the first lunar landing module. And, as far as computers are concerned, change is one thing, but the current rate of obsolescence bothers the hell out of me. In fact, I'm at the point where I absolutely refuse to buy another piece of technology until they promise me that they will stop inventing new stuff. My stockbroker (that word "broker" should have been a clue) even told me that soon we'll be able to buy and sell stocks at neighborhood ATM machines—which is good I guess as it will give muggers a chance to diversify their portfolios.

In any event, winners know that a company, an organization, an industry, or an individual's ability to recognize change and then to react quickly and appropriately to that change is the key to staying on top. They also know, however, that it's much, much easier to *get* on top than it is to *stay* there. Staying on top requires not only seeing change and responding to it; it involves embracing change, keenly adopting change, and eagerly assimilating it.

Winners know that even if you're on a winning track —if you don't shift your position on that track, sooner or later you'll get hit by a speeding train. Being able to change your perspective and remain flexible makes you a key asset in today's fast-paced business world. Yes, if you live in the past today, your life will quickly become ancient history. Winners know this; losers often design their own extinction. By being masters at change, winners know that when they see the light at the end of the tunnel, it will not be the light of an oncoming train.

Change however, offers us another challenge, as it's more than embracing the new; it's eliminating the old. Alvin Toffler, the wise and eloquent futurist, said that the illiterate of the future will not be those who cannot read or write, but instead those who cannot unlearn and relearn.

The CEO of a Fortune 500 company in Pittsburgh recently told me that he was involved with his company in an executive position for 39 years. He then added that unfortunately most of what he's learned is quite simply no longer relevant. He agrees with current business pundits who hold that it is far easier to take a company down than to change it. He told me that one of his personal obstacles is deleting from his mind what no longer works. Yes, he elaborated that coming up with new ideas and understanding new changes is not the issue, as much as letting go of what once worked but is now obsolete. Years ago, Satchel Paige said that it's not what you don't know that will hurt you, as much as what you know that's no longer so.

Price Pritchett, in his insightful handbooks on change, says that human beings are regularity-seeking animals. Regularity is familiar, adaptive, and efficient. In fact, some of us actually value regularity in our lives even more than we value life itself. Yes, some people would rather die than change. Right now, I have a business associate who was diagnosed with a serious disease. Amazingly, he knows his physician is not the best in the field but he just doesn't want to go through the hassle of finding a better one. Come on, we're talking life and death here.

There are four basic types of changes that we encounter in our lives:

1. *Changes that we anticipate and want to occur.* Examples of this are accepting a new job offer, making a new friend, seizing a travel opportunity.

2. *Changes that we anticipate will happen but don't particularly want to occur.* Examples of this are unexpectedly having to buy a new car, going to the doctor for treatment, adjusting to a new boss.

3. *Changes we don't anticipate will happen but would like to occur.* Examples of this are winning the lottery, being asked to spearhead a new division of your company, finding a Picasso in your grandmother's attic.

4. *Changes we don't anticipate will happen and don't want to occur.* Examples of this are enduring a serious illness, learning your pension plan has been depleted through company mismanagement, suddenly losing a loved one.

Change is a part of life. If you don't change, you don't grow. The fact of the matter is that **if you don't make changes, change will happen to you.** And when change happens to you, you're not in control. Most people are reactive to change; winners are proactive with change — winners like to be in control.

Unfortunately, even positive, relatively easy change can be extremely difficult to make. Change puts us on unfamiliar ground. I've seen people in organizations not only resist change, but actually get enraged about it. Their attitude seems to stem from one or several of these six fears:

1. *Fear of the unknown.* We all know that familiarity breeds content. The Deutsch Group of management consultants say that fear of the unknown is the single biggest factor in resisting change.

2. *Fear of failure.* The learning curve surely involves some setbacks. Since it took so much time to master our current skills, we find starting anew to be not only disheartening but to pose an opportunity for failure.

3. *Fear of success.* Success comes with its own demands. Staying successful takes work. When we have success opportunities, we see that there are no victims, just volunteers. No longer are there excuses to be cynical or negative.

4. *Fear of commitment.* Decisions are easy to make — they are logical, rational, intellectual. Productive change, on the other hand, requires commitment. Commitments are hard to make because they involve emotions. Getting emotionally involved takes dedication, passion, and work.

5. *Fear of disapproval.* Change not only affects your life; it may affect the lives of others in your close circle. Perhaps your friends or family will be intolerant, skeptical, or unsupportive. So change may in fact place more demands on them as well. Perhaps you feel that

you can't rock the boat and make others unhappy. Often we value other people's opinions more than our own. The *disease to please* can prove devastating, and throw you off your winning course.

6. *Fear of confusion.* Just when you were starting to really get it and breeze through certain aspects of your job, uncertainty comes calling and order falls away. Having order and confidence eliminates that feeling of embarrassment and confusion. With change in the air, order and confidence are often lost for a while.

Yes, change is a part of growing and we must fight the human instinct to keep the status quo. If we deny change, we become stagnant. No matter how hard you try to be a winner, you can't freeze-frame your life. Once you really understand that principle and become receptive and re-teachable, you will note that fear starts diminishing.

Since change is not an obstacle to overcome but a process to embrace, it is best to change before you're forced into it. Examine the ways you think and act and consider modifying them to help effect change in yourself as well as in the lives of others.

When trying to execute change and meeting resistance from others, you must:

1. *Realize that people tend to support what they had a hand in creating.* Therefore, those who you want to change must be made to feel that they have some voice in the upcoming change.

2. *Make certain that those who must change are not kept in the dark.* Gather people as a group so everyone is hearing the same thing at the same time. This is critical, in that mutual understanding of what that change entails, quells rumors and uneasiness.

3. *Always begin by giving the big-change picture first.* People digest and learn information best when it is presented from the broad to the specific. Without apologies or preliminary explanations, state clearly what change is going to be made. Start with the *what*.

4. *Then move on to the why.* Explain why this decision to change has been made. Note some of the negative repercussions of not changing. **This is where you sell it!**

5. *Move on to the how.* Explain how this change will benefit the company, and if possible how the change will benefit people individually. Most are still interested in knowing what's in it for them.

6. *Before you progress to the when you expect the changes to start occurring, take the time to demonstrate your awareness of your team's feelings.* Though a timetable must be set, it is imperative that you exhibit empathy for the feelings of others and assure them that they will have adequate time to understand, adjust to, become more comfortable with, and become more adept at handling the new changes. Point out the difference between the real outcome of the change and their feelings about the change. Their acceptance

will have little to do with the extent of the change and more to do with the sensitivity and compassion you demonstrate during its presentation.

7. *If warranted, discuss what new training will take place to prepare the team for the change.* Be specific here, as it will calm many anxieties.

8. *Since change does not just happen overnight, talk about how the change will progress.* It is important to tie in the present with the future. Use verbiage such as, "Here is where we are now, today, and this is where we want to be by such-and-such a date." Again, a timetable is critical in giving people transition-target dates.

9. *Then proceed by asking for the team's suggestions and ideas relative to how they feel the change could be best executed.* This step again serves to bring the team into the picture and help them to feel involved. Phony participation will only make the change more difficult to implement. The team's interest and enthusiasm will grow as they are encouraged to express their ideas. A change in behavior begins with a change in one's mind. This step starts that process.

10. *Point out areas that will not be affected by the change.* For many, this creates a psychological comfort zone.

11. *Be up front.* Talk about the positives as well as some of the potential pitfalls of the changes. Coming forth with both sides in advance eliminates a good portion of the disappointment and distress when glitches happen.

12. *Celebrate the change.*

Now, if your personal attitude toward change is not as accepting or as fast as it should be, here are some suggestions to get **YOU** going personally in a positive direction.

- *Acknowledge that you may have self-defeating justification for not changing, and decline to give in to them.* Acknowledge that, though so much of change can't be controlled, you can control your attitude about change.

- *Remember that if you don't like what you're getting, you have to change what you're doing.*

- *Repeat these four phrases several times during the course of the day:*

  - I want to move into the future.

  - I will be open to learning as well as personal and professional development.

  - I am a forward-thinking person.

  - I am taking action steps to keep current, to advance and to keep winning in life.

- *Think in terms of "I can learn" instead of "I already know."*

- *Understand that, though it is perfectly acceptable to visit the past, you can't live there.* Remember from previous chapters that pessimistic people tend to stay in the past. Winners are future-directed and tend to be more optimistic.

- *Recognize that change is a life-long process.*

- *When you start something new, don't expect perfection.* Understand that mistakes will happen as part of the change process.

- *Always begin with a step that will bring you perceptible results no matter how seemingly small that step is.*

- *Bring some familiarity into a changing situation.* For example, if you are changing offices try to keep the furniture arrangement as it once was for a while. If you are moving to a new city, seek out some of the chain stores you frequented before. If you are changing jobs, place familiar photos out on your new desk. Put the same art on the wall that you had before.

- *Avoid temptation to turn back to the old way unless you see clearly and undeniably that the new change has nothing to offer.*

- *Stick more fervently to your positive daily routines.* Don't skip that morning run, that glass of wine while making dinner, or that evening bubble bath.

- *Search for others who have made similar changes.* Their support can help you immensely. For example, if you have moved abroad, find others from your area who are living there. If you are suddenly put in a managerial position, join a management group or become affiliated with a management association to meet others in your position. If you're changing your eating habits, connect with others who are eating the way you do now. All this helps you adjust to change.

- *Commit to becoming more flexible and mobile.* The phrase "It's not my job" has most definitely left the building.

- *Be more accepting of ambiguity and vagueness.* When change is afoot, attempting to see where you fit in, initially, may be like trying to nail Silly String to the wall. Relinquish the need for excess structure at this time. You will eventually create role-clarity for yourself.

- *In rapidly changing times, experience is not what it used to be.* Current performance is what matters. Remember it's your contribution now that will make you worthwhile.

- *Start practicing kaizen.* It's a Japanese term meaning a relentless quest for a better way.

- *Since problems are an expected and likely offspring of change, commit to being a fixer rather than a blamer.* Think about solutions not problems.

- *Keep your expectations high but get the concept of entitlement out of your mind.* Remember that in today's changing business culture, you can't maintain your reputation based on what you once did.

Corporate America is proof that past reputation does not guarantee ongoing success.

The ability to change is tied into survival. Treat change as a welcomed guest in your life. As my grandma said, "When you're done changing, you're done."

Chapter

12

Winning Principle

Winners Know the E-ssentials of Success

Winners know that especially in the workplace there are euphemisms that are widely used to make things sound better, nicer, less offensive, and more palatable than they really are. For example:

"Be a part of our fast-paced company" has come to usually mean, "Hey, we have no time to train you. From day one, you're out there on your own."

"We offer a competitive salary" most likely translates as, "The only way we can compete in the marketplace is to pay our employees less than our competition pays theirs."

"We're looking for people with a wide variety of experience who are adept at multi-tasking" is telling you that they're looking for someone to replace two people who just quit and two others who were just fired.

"Must be a quick study and deadline-oriented" probably means "From your very first day on the job, you'll be at least eight weeks behind."

"Seeking individuals with leadership skills" can almost certainly be interpreted as, "You'll have the responsibilities of a manager, without the salary, respect, authority, or power."

"Seeking quality, well-rounded individuals with more than a high level of intelligence" is telling you that "Extensive experience, smarts, and a high IQ in the field are not going to be enough to get our attention. We want more. We want candidates with energy, ethics, enthusiasm, elevated expectations, and an equalized (or controlled) ego."

Yes, many outstanding companies today are aware of the fact that there is much more to on-the-job success and effectiveness than one's sheer intellect and experience in the field. Smart companies look also for a high EQ (or a high emotional quotient) in potential employees.

Employees who have a high EQ have an elevated degree of emotional intelligence: They have brain power, are better team players, are more productive, raise the company bar, enhance the work environment, bring a sense of responsibility, stability, and commitment to the workplace—and reduce costly turnover.

A number of factors comprise one's EQ, and a number of experts keep sorting out exactly what they are. Universally, it seems, however, that gauging one's inner self and assessing one's feelings and reactions, as well as delving into what one stands for and what one values, all contribute to determining that measure.

The emotional aspect of success is something that winners have long realized. From Robert Cooper's breakthrough work on emotional intelligence to Janelle Barlow's insightful book explaining the importance of providing customers and clients with something called "emotional value"—the emotional extension of the word motion—has become an important consideration for top companies and for top employees worldwide.

Yes, a person who can perform, move, do the job with more than smarts but with solid sense, stability, sensitivity, standards, and savvy has become a much-sought-after corporate commodity.

Though, as I mentioned, there may be differing opinions as to what elements constitute EQ, I have formulated my own E-list. This list consists of the characteristics or traits that winners have that serve to support the fact that it's more than smarts that gets you, and keeps you, on top. These elements are what I have dubbed some of the E-ssential elements of being emotionally appealing to a company, organization, or in fact to any other worthwhile human beings. They are the elements of:

- Energy
- Elevated expectations
- Ethics
- Emotional stability
- Enthusiasm
- Equalized ego

Winners have repeatedly confirmed that these elements in proper proportion have enabled them to be grounded with the solid principles that separate them from the ordinary—and that have played a major role in their ongoing success. In today's world, these elements will definitely serve to make you unique.

Energy

Energy is truly the magic elixir. It's been called the fuel of life, and there is no doubt in my mind that the world belongs to the energetic. Winners have energy. In fact, many winners possess the maximum amount of energy allowed without government regulations. You could never call a winner passive, you could never call them a follower or re-active. Winners know that everything has happened and will continue to happen because of a thing called energy. Winners are well aware that life did not materialize be-cause matter was mellow and DNA was passive. Energy was at the start of it all. In fact, the energy that winners bring to the table usually excites, entices, and ignites the energy of others. Energy is indeed contagious and, of course, so is lack of it. Winners know that energy must be in continuous supply. . .

- As jobs become more ambiguous.
- As more flexibility is now a requirement of the work-place.
- As work that is "worth paying for" becomes almost a corporate mantra.
- As the words "owed" and "entitled to" must be omit-ted from one's vocabulary.
- As customers get more savvy and better informed.
- As customers' expectations keep rising.
- As clients become more demanding.
- And as you're only as good as what you're doing at this very moment.

Yes winners know that they have to be "bold, they have to be bad, they have to be wiser. They have to be hard, they have to be tough, they have to be stronger. They have to be cool, they have to be calm, they have to stay together." (I wish I just made that up.) However, when Desiree sang those words, she belted them out with the emphasis they deserve.

All the above take energy. Therefore, one of your tasks in developing that winning way is to find out what gives you energy. THINK:

- What do I do that gets me feeling energized?
- What do I do that seems to get me going?
- What do I do that makes me feel I could go on forever?

Perhaps it's working in your garden or playing chess, talking to a particular person, reading a certain type of book, playing squash, shopping, or studying maps. Winners know how to generate energy when they need it. They have recognized their energy sources and tap into them frequently.

Winners know that when you give into laziness, you surrender control over your life. They also know that laziness is an easy trap. Isn't it obvious that as a society we have become more lazy? I know people who, after going to the dry cleaners, have to take a nap before they make their next stop at the bank. And I really can't believe that people are microwaving Pop Tarts. How lazy is that?

Energy gets you up, it invigorates you, it enlivens you, it makes your senses sharper. Nietzsche said, "Never trust an idea that comes upon you when you're sitting down." It takes a good deal of energy today to think as productively and creatively as you must. John Le Carre echoed those sentiments when he said, "The desk is a dangerous place from which to watch the world."

In any event, whether your goal is to be a winning employee or a winning employer, it takes energy to influence and lead others. One of the most important obligations of all great leaders begins with determining how to raise their own personal energy level, so that they can then choreograph and stir up the energies of all others around them.

Elevated Expectations

Winners know that in life you don't get what you want; you only get what you expect. Accordingly, winners have high expectations. I had lunch with an old acquaintance recently who just never seemed to advance in life; she feels stuck and in the "same old grind," as she put it. For clarification and perhaps to get her to think, I asked her what she wants in life. Beside the answers of health, happiness, love, and friendship, she mentioned that she also wanted a nice home; a new (instead of her usual used) car; and a small horse farm. Then I asked the next logical question. "Do you feel that you'll eventually have those things?" Her sarcastic response said it all, "Sure, right. Me? Are you kidding?" I can guarantee that she will never have those things because she has not taken the first winning step toward having them—expecting them.

There is a philosophy that I learned about back in the 1960s when I taught sixth grade in Orange, New Jersey at the unconventional and well-respected Nassau School. It was called the philosophy of imputation. That philosophy refers to the fact that people tend to perform according to what's expected of them. That holds true for your expectations of others as well as for your expectations of yourself.

To get this point across, our school psychologist told us the story about a rookie teacher who, of course, was given the kids that no other teacher wanted. At the end of the year, she received special recognition for making the most progress with a class and having the largest jump in standardized test scores from the beginning of the year to the end. When receiving this award at a banquet, she said that she had an unfair advantage because the kids she was given as a new teacher were so incredibly smart to begin with. The head of the board of education looked at her as if she was crazy and interrupted, asking her why she felt they were so smart. She answered that when given her class roster on that first day the IQ scores that appeared next to each student's name were all far above average. With that, the entire audience started laughing, as it was explained that those numbers were not IQ scores but locker numbers.

So what do you expect from yourself and from others? Winners know that it's easy to initially start out a venture with high expectations; the tough part is keeping those expectations high as you progress. Unfortunately, you see, we have a tendency to change our expectations. Think about it. You have a baby. You hold that baby in your arms and you think, "Ah, this baby is going to grow up to be a Rhodes scholar, perhaps a Nobel Prize-winning physicist or the ambassador to Switzerland." (I'm trying to pick a neutral country here.) Then, after many years pass, one day you look at that grown-up baby out of the corner of your eye and you think, "Hell, well at least he's not on drugs." Yes, so many people change their expectations. Winners, however, not only start out with high expectations—they keep them high and don't allow them to slide.

To help your expectations reach fruition, ask yourself these three questions:

- What is the very best thing that could happen to me, my family, and my company this year?

- What are the worse things that could happen to me, my family, and my company this year?

- What can I start doing immediately to ensure that the best things will indeed happen, and the worst things will not?

Then you must, as a winner, follow through by taking action. Commit to taking one step each and every day (in terms of yourself, your family, and your company) that will lead you closer to making sure that the best things will indeed happen and the worse things won't. Of course, there are some things in life we can't control; however, winners like to control what they can.

Ethics

Some people find it hard to differentiate between morals and ethics. It has been said that morals are of a more personal nature and ethics are more business related. In any event, they are the principles you live by, and when your principles are clear to you, your goals, objectives and purpose in life have a tendency to become clear as well.

Your ethics serve as your conscience. Your ethics consist of your personal sense of honor and integrity. It can't be denied that ostensibly winning without ethics and honor has happened to some. Yes, some have attained success without much, or perhaps without any, emphasis on personal ethics. While success without ethics might satisfy the ego, I am willing to bet big bucks that it just doesn't taste that sweet. Tony Soprano sees a psychiatrist regularly, because though he has the power he wants, it just doesn't feel as good as it should.

Sam Hill of Helios Consulting in New York said, "The work ethic may not be dead; it just may be retired, wearing plaid pants, and playing golf in Palm Springs." He intimated that finding ethical talent today is not an easy task for companies. He elaborated that with an economic downturn or not, talent with a strong work ethic in Corporate America is in very short supply. In fact, he even warned employers to expect to pay a premium to recruit and keep such talent.

Taking all that into consideration, I advise people looking for work to make certain that during job interviews, they always bring up the issues of loyalty, honesty, and integrity. They must sell their personal ethics as they would any other more skill-based asset. Winners do this naturally because they are well aware of the contribution high ethics brings to any situation.

I'm certain that you have heard stories, especially today in light of the investigations into unethical behavior in Corporate America, about the scarcity of ethics. My favorite one is about Ralph who believed that virtue really was its own reward. Ralph always acted ethically in his business as well as in his personal life. When he died, God himself met Ralph at the Pearly Gates. "Are you hungry?" asked God. "Sure," responded Ralph. After all, it had been a long trip. So God opened a can of tuna fish and a box of Ritz crackers for them to share. While they were enjoying the snack, Ralph looked down into Hell and noticed that the folks there were having filet mignon, champagne, pâté, and caviar. Ralph turned to God and asked, "Why do the people in Hell get a feast and all we get up here in Heaven is tuna fish and Ritz crackers?" And God said, "Well, quite frankly with just the two of us up here, I didn't feel that it paid to cook."

Winners know that pure intentions do matter, and that they do go hand-in-hand with the good feelings that winners have. Winners, in fact, seem to hold themselves responsible to a higher standard. As Harper Lee said in *To Kill a Mockingbird*, "The one thing that does not abide by majority rule is a person's conscience."

Winners know how to stand their ground, especially if someone presents them with an offer, a deal, or something that just does not feel ethically correct. They simply echo or rephrase the words that Rob Roy gave us in the movies, "You underestimate me. Honor is the gift I give myself."

Emotional Stability

Ann Landers once said that one person out of every three is mentally imbalanced. Using this statistic to make a point, I often ask my audiences to glance to their right and then to their left, stating that if those other two people look okay, they had better start worrying about themselves! The fact of the matter is that being able to demonstrate emotional stability is a valuable asset in today's world, where everything that once was a sin seems to now be a disease.

In any event, winners do indeed know that when working, they have to leave their problems behind. That old cliché—"If you're ever inclined to tell others your problems, remember 50 percent of the people you tell won't care, and the other 50 percent believe you deserve to have those problems."

Being emotionally stable does not mean being problem free. It means being able to have discretion; it means knowing when and when not to talk about your problems.

Then, it involves solving them on your own time while still being able to move forward during that solving process. Winners can separate; they know that since they spend nearly 60 percent of their lives either getting ready for work, actually at work, or trying to get over what happened at work. Keeping their problems in perspective is as critical as not sharing them with the world.

Enthusiasm

Though I have talked about enthusiasm in some of the previous chapters, I must reiterate its importance in winning. I tell my clients that they must insist on it from their employees. I remind them that employee enthusiasm gives the customer faith in the company, and that it has been proven that people usually judge a company, or an establishment of any kind, based on the level of enthusiasm of those who work there.

Recently my husband and I went out to celebrate a major anniversary. We made reservations at one of the newest and supposedly best restaurants in Washington, D.C., and were prepared to spend some "change" there. I started dieting early on in the week to bank my calories, so to speak, so I could indulge myself during that special night. We were both really looking forward to this evening.

Upon arriving at the restaurant, we were greeted by the maitre d' who had obviously confused class with aloofness. Be that as it may, we knew that he was going to be out of our lives the moment he seated us. However, then came the waiter. Now, a waiter can make or break one's dining experience, and this guy definitely broke ours. He had a superior attitude from the get-go, never smiled, rarely made eye contact, and rattled off the chef's specials as if he was bored with the entire scenario and had somewhere else to go. He clearly thought that he was the best thing the restaurant had to offer and didn't have one ounce of enthusiasm for anything on the menu.

Though the dinner was acceptable, clearly we will never return to this establishment. Being a speaker, I also have the pleasure of being able to spread the word about it. However, even now, I still think of how that waiter's lack of enthusiasm affected everything. His lack of enthusiasm got us wondering how good could this place be if the people here have no enthusiasm for it.

Winners know that enthusiasm is not a random mood; it is, in fact, an everyday choice. Winners know that though they can't always wake up feeling bright-eyed, bushy-tailed, and enthusiastic, they do indeed have the capacity to fake it—and they do.

Equalized Ego

For some, after they reach a modicum of success, after they win a few awards, earn a big bonus, or receive accolades from their bosses, their egos get the best of them and take over. They even perhaps start thinking that they're superior to others. They think they're untouchable.

For some, success can easily breed a loss of humility. Ted Turner was quoted once as saying, "If I only had a little humility, I'd be perfect." Yes, with success one can lose humility and perspective. The future from that point on is usually downhill. Therefore, winners know that though it is wonderful to revel in the success they have earned, they must never forget who they are and where they came from.

Now, belief in yourself is critical. It not only further motivates you but gets other to believe in you as well. So, listen to the voice within you, but through balance and hard work make certain you don't believe every single thing you hear. Remember, everyone who got to where they are began where they once were. And to avoid going back, heed the words of Peggy Fleming's mother after her daughter's success in the Olympics. "Always believe in yourself, but never, ever believe your own PR."

Chapter

13

Winning Principle

*Winners Have Snap-back-ability and
Know How to Get Out of a Slump*

Slumps happen. High and low cycles are part of the rhythm of life, be it your home life or your work life. And yes, from time to time bad things do indeed happen to good people.

Though winners don't expect slumps or low cycles, they do indeed know how to get over them if they happen. Winners know how to override obstacles to keep them on top of their game, and they know how to minimize their downtime by being slump busters and having snapback-ability.

Many things, of course, can lead to slumps in the business world. Poor market conditions, new competition, a slow economy, resting on your laurels, taking success for granted, personal burn out, a series of disappointments, and, believe it or not, even good market conditions can lead to slumps.

Yes, a slump is not always a sign of bad times. In fact, the term slump usually refers to producing low or no results when market conditions indicate that those results should be higher. Of course, when that slump happens with no ostensible outside cause, concern, self-doubt, frustration, anxiety, and introspection often enter the picture—and the bummer is that those things can get you into an even deeper slump.

Though winners, of course, do look at slump situations with an analytical mind, they also know that to control their own destiny they must be able to get out of that slump, whatever the cause, on their own and as quickly as possible. They must develop slump resistance and snapback-ability. They must rise above and overcome it all. Yes, winners understand slumps. They understand that they can happen for a variety of reasons other than a low business cycle. For example, there are:

Burn-out Slumps: Feeling burned out can happen to anyone. Of course to be truly burned out, remember, you once had to be on fire, so winners know that there is indeed a difference between being burned out and being rusted out. Contrary to what most people think, however, burnout does not come from hard work. Burnout comes from frustration. So winners take the time to identify the source of their frustration. Frustration can emanate from poor communication, too much red tape, lack of follow-through from others, dedication without appreciation, responsibility without authority, and so on. If untreated, this type of frustration leads to burnout, which then can lead to a slump. Winners set out to analyze if they are currently in a frustration situation, they determine the source of that frustration, and then they commit to either minimizing or fixing it.

Lack-of-Challenge Slumps: These types of slumps happen if the work you are doing on a day-to-day basis begins to offer little or no challenge. Yes, to many people the challenge is what turns them on, and if the work comes all too easily, boredom and disinterest set in. A feeling of, "Heck, anyone can do this job," can manifest itself in a performance slump. Yes, having to work hard at a task often provides a motivational impetus for many to stay on the top of their game. Once they can win without much effort, they simply lose the edge. Losing the edge can soon turn into that slump. Winners who like the challenge recognize when success is coming too easily for them. Then, they make every effort to seek out new challenges that serve to show them how good they really are.

Contest, Crises, or Goal Slumps: I have noted that quite often when a contest within a company has just been completed, when a crises within an organization has just been resolved, or when goals have just been met, there is a pervasive, overall slump that invades many of the employees. You see, it's human nature to feel, "Hell, we did the job they wanted. We overcame the crises. Our division won the contest. We met our goals. Now, we deserve to lie back, revel in our success, and let it all slide a while."

I always tell my clients to beware of the times when those hurdles have been overcome, or when the expectations have been met. Usually, a performance slowdown is in the works — and employees feel justified in a diluted effort since they worked so hard to turn things around, work through the crunch, or reach those ambitious goals.

These are the times that serious motivation and new challenges have to be brought into the picture. These are the times when management has to really be on top of it all; these are the times when winners are the most cautious, because they know that it's often hard to rekindle efforts *after* a slowdown. I'm not advising companies to avoid contests and the like; I'm just warning you to be aware of the situation they often create. Winners are aware of these scenarios and the potential pitfalls that can follow.

Good-Time Slumps: Yes, there are unfortunately many perils of a good market. A good market can cover up a great many bad things, and all too often, poor personal performance is one of those bad things. You see, in very good times, it's usually easy to make money without having to go through all the usual machinations. In good times, you can skip some of the steps that originally made you successful. In good times, you can get a bit sloppy and still succeed. The fact that good times breed bad habits eludes us. But it's a fact that prevents many occasional winners from being consistent winners.

Perhaps it's human nature to work only as hard as you have to. As so many behavioral scientists have noted, human beings have an amazing ability to stretch themselves when need be and also have the ability to recoil at the slightest provocation.

If success keeps happening and money continues to flow, it almost seems stupid to bust your chops, to do more than it actually takes, or to go the extra mile. The problem with that thinking, however, revolves around the issue of habits. Consistent winning is about habits, and when an attitude, approach, or behavior is no longer practiced on a regular basis, it no longer classifies as a habit.

So, big deal, you skip some steps, you cut a few corners. What's the harm? The trouble is that we often lose sight of how far we've deviated from the right way of doing things. You see, even in good times, a work-level threshold must be met, or else the bottom-line starts suffering. The problem is, it's hard to determine that point. So, sooner or later, even the good times' success factor is affected and compromised by sloppy habits, and before you know it, yes, that bottom-line starts to suffer.

I recall, just recently, talking to a salesperson who was making great money working for a food distributor in Atlanta. "The market was great," he said, "I could actually almost just take orders, and I figured it was stupid to knock my socks off and go through all the normal paces if I could still make money leapfrogging with the selling system."

This worked well for a while, he told me, but not for long. Soon, he got completely out of the habit of doing it the right way. Then, when he realized he had abandoned the system too much and had to reincorporate the missing steps back into his presentation because of a market slowdown, he downright resented it. That resentment not only affected his performance, but also was telegraphed to his suppliers and purchasers. That led to a fast downward spiral that took quite a long time to mend.

Winning and success are about habits and doing what you have to do, even when you don't have to do it. Repetition and commitment to those habits are the only things that lead to consistent winning. Habits are persistence in practice.

Disappointment Slumps: Now, let's lay the cards on the table. People have disappointment in their lives. Anyone who says otherwise is either just not telling the truth or holds very low expectations. Disappointments happen, but several successively or within a short period of time can lead to a slump. Disappointments can pile up, because people don't know how to handle them as they come—and then move on. In many instances, visibly reacting to a disappointment in public demonstrates to others your vulnerability. This could damage others' perception of your emotional fortitude and hurt you in the future. On the other hand, if you keep it all inside, it can fester, grow, and eventually drown you. As Dr. Abraham Zaleznik from Harvard said, "Many people are trapped by disappointment." Yes, to some, even a single disappointment can be the start of a slump.

Recognize the Source of Your Slump

Yes, you must recognize the source of your slump and then turn to these slump busters to help you get back to where you want to be as quickly as possible—and on your own.

1. *Examine your feelings.* Don't run away from them. Allow yourself some time to ponder what occurred, and sift through what happened to you as a result. Acknowledge disappointment, frustration, and even con-

fusion. It's okay to feel bad about hitting a slump. It would be dangerous not to. Being well adjusted does not mean being able to live with slumps while not getting upset about them. However, don't dwell on those negative feelings. Instead, think about what you can learn from the situation. Slumps happen for a reason, and if you can figure out what you've been doing wrong, or what market forces you failed to anticipate, you can benefit from the experience and be better prepared next time. Learn from the slump and grow from the experience. The key is to work through it and not to shelve it. You must come to terms with it, but you must also be committed to moving on. If it remains harbored in your head, it will most definitely lead to cynicism. And cynicism is more than debilitating: It is unhealthy. So, put aside some time to think about that slump; then do everything in your power to let it go and move on.

2. *Talk about your slump with a trusted friend, colleague, or coworker.* Communicate to them that your goal is to accentuate the positives and put the negatives behind you, but that as a part of your snap-back process you would like to articulate the situation and your feelings. Once you've put it into words, however, stop talking about it. If you have no one you feel you can talk to, then write those feelings down. Yes, put your thoughts on paper. Often, just by talking it through, or writing it down, you will clearly see what needs to be done to fix it.

3. *Start separating your ego from your loss.* Remember, just because you've lost some customers doesn't mean you've lost your skill and ability to find new ones. Though perhaps you've lost some money-making opportunities, you've not lost your capacity to take advantage of other similar opportunities that will come along. Remember that no matter what you lost during this slump, nothing and no one can turn you into a loser without your agreement and approval. Don't be disappointed with yourself.

4. *Engage in a process or system reorientation.* Break down the fundamental tasks involved in your job. Make up your mind to perform your job one day at a time. Be honest with yourself. Ask yourself some tough questions. Have those fundamentals slipped? Have I started to ignore the relationship aspect of my job? Am I really being as proactive as I need to be, or is my initiative level down? Am I actually asking for business? Am I following through as diligently as I should? Am I just going through the motions—and failing to analyze my actions to see if they will produce the results I want? This is the time to reflect. Isolate the areas of your job that you have been neglecting, and refocus to give them some special attention.

5. *Prospect for new customers, reconnect with your marginal customers, and find some new allies.* Ask current customers for referrals, commit to holding the hand of that marginal prospect a little more, and get out there

to meet people who share your values. You don't need someone who plays devil's advocate now. Remember your positive, healing actions today will determine the results you have tomorrow.

6. *Use the extra time you now have to get organized, clean out files, study up on the competition, and learn more about those you partner with.* Perhaps take a course, read a new business book, listen to a new tape series. In other words, polish up your knowledge base, and organizational methods.

7. *Experiment and try some new approaches when working with your clients and customers.* Perhaps add a few new words to your vocabulary, find a new story to tell that will get that important point across, change your modus operandi in some way. Get out of that rut, because if you're sleepwalking through your work, you must change something about it to wake you up. Just by changing what you normally do will most likely rejuvenate your presentation, attitude, and perspective. Remember, change keeps you on the edge. Though you of course want that edge to be leading—not bleeding—it's been said that if you aren't on the edge, you're taking up too much space.

8. *Since your work mood, energy level, and success factor is affected by your home life, commit to finishing some project you've been putting off on the home front.* Once you get around to finishing that project you've been neglecting, you'll have a sense of accomplishment

that will keep your ego afloat and remind you of how capable you really are. That little jolt of off-the-job success is often just the ticket you need to get back on track on the job.

9. *Jump-start your attitude.* You'll have an easier time getting out of a slump if your attitude is not stuck there too. Besides hanging around with those friends and colleagues that will give you a boost, reread those great testimonials and references you have received over the years. Even call upon some more recent people you have worked with to add a few new glowing letters to your collection. That step will help remind you of how good you really are.

10. *Remember personal improvement leads to professional improvement.* Therefore take advantage of inspirational material available on the market. Familiarize yourself with stories of famous winners who turned a situation that seemed discouraging or bleak into an incredible victory or accomplishment. Reconnect with your role models, mentors, and the people who inspire you. Find your spirituality and bring it back into your daily life.

11. *Accept those party and social invitations even if you have to literally force yourself to go.* Expand your network. Connections with people represent opportunities. Remember it's not about how many people you know: It's about how many people know you. The more people who know you, the more likely they or

someone they know will want to do business with you. Get out and about.

12. *Evaluate your physical shape?* As Lucy Ricardo so eloquently said, "Are you tired, listless? Do you poop out at parties?" Remember expending energy begets more energy. Often, just by getting your exercise routine back in order, your success will follow suite. Yes, work slumps often occur when we get lax in taking care of our physical shape.

13. *Recheck the balance in your life.* Sigmund Freud said that the emotionally healthy person develops three abilities in life—the ability to love, to work, and to play. You will most definitely lower your risk of getting in a slump if your balance between work, family, and play is right.

14. *Check out your goals in all areas of your life.* Rethink your priorities. Remember goals need deadlines—are yours set and realistic? Are you doing at least one thing each day to get you closer to at least one of your goals? Also, make your goals even more short-term at this time.

15. *Don't be afraid to let go of a goal, or change a goal that has been bringing you repeated disappointment and frustration.* Sometimes you have to let it go, or change your perspective to get there. When Thomas Edison set out to invent the light bulb, he didn't do it by trying to improve on the candle. Take time to think. A moment's insight can often save you a lifetime of hassle, disappointment, and discouragement.

16. *Rank your ability to get those new wins.* This will help you climb out of that slump. In other words, if you're working with a new customer or client, try to assign them a rating number based on what your chances of success with them will be. An excellent opportunity for success with them would be an "A" rating, pretty good would be a "B," fair a "C," and slim a "D." If you have an overwhelming number of "A's" in your pool, you may be setting yourself up for a continued slump or another slump based on unrealistic expectations that can turn into disappointments. Being optimistic is essential, but so is being realistic.

17. *Count your blessings.* Make thankfulness a daily habit, especially now. Often just that simple act can help you see things more clearly and put things in a better, more empowering perspective.

The point is this, when you hit a dry spell, don't panic. Slumps are inevitable, common and temporary. The key is to minimize your downtime. Winners use these steps to help them do just that.

Chapter
14

Winning Principle

*Winners Are Willing to Do What
It Takes to Get What They Want*

Being a speaker, I have the greatest job in the world for a woman: I talk and get paid for it. I can literally talk for hours on any given subject—and if I know anything at all about the subject, I can go on for days, weeks, months. I think my gift of gab was inherited from my father, a very successful CPA with 3 offices. He loved to tell stories to his family as well as his clients, and he would talk for hours about the opportunities that living in America afforded. From early on, he drilled into me that people each and every day, from all over the world, are clawing to get to America for the amazing opportunities that exist here. He explained that people are not plotting to get into Russia or conniving to get into Somalia; opportunities are limited there, at least the legal ones.

Along with this message, my father told me a story about his father coming to America—again for the opportunities. I've since heard from others that they too heard the same story, in one form or another, about one of their ancestors. Knowing how my father told his stories to get a point across in a nonacademic way, its familial authenticity is in question, but the point is right on.

I learned that Grandpa came from the Old Country (not Busch Gardens, the real Old Country). When the boat docked at Ellis Island, Grandpa had to go through the frustrating, arduous, exhausting, and, of course, perplexing immigration process. Once that was completed, rather than feeling drained or exhausted, he felt invigorated, alive and excited to be in America, the land of opportunity.

Grandpa then made his way into downtown Manhattan to find the apartment belonging to the people he would live with until he could get his feet on the ground. However, in awe of the city, he wandered around the streets of New York for several hours first, just taking it all in.

After a while, Grandpa got hungry (I inherited that trait from him). So, the story has it, he walked another few blocks and found himself in front of a cafeteria-type restaurant. Watching for a while, he got the drift. Yes, Grandpa realized that the food here would be relatively inexpensive, so he went in and sat down at a table. Of course, he had no idea how a cafeteria worked, so he just sat and waited for someone to come along and serve him. After sitting there for quite a while, waiting for that waitress to come along, a gentleman at a nearby table offered Grandpa assistance. The man told Grandpa that all he had to do was to stand up, get a tray, go through the line, decide what he wanted, take it, and then just pay for it.

Supposedly, Grandpa later said that that experience was his first taste of America, and to him it was symbolic. To him, that typified what America was all about. In America, you can have anything you want— anything you want along the line—as long as you're willing to pay for it. Grandpa, by the way, decided that he wanted to become a successful businessman. He paid for his success by putting in long hours, becoming an apprentice, working three jobs at once, and spending hours upon hours learning English and reading.

When my father first told me Grandpa's story, I really didn't care much about the message, and actually didn't even get (or pay attention to) the point. But, as I got older, that message became an important one in my life.

Yes, winners:

1. Recognize the opportunity that America offers.

2. Know that they can have nearly anything they want— if they're willing to pay the price for it.

3. Understand that the price often includes the commitment to do more than your best—but to do what it takes.

Interestingly enough, many people however, don't even know what it is that they want. There are too many "ifs," "ands" and "buts" in their equation. Perhaps it's too complex a question to even ponder. For some, they feel it's too late to think about it; for others, it's too depressing a thought to even entertain. But, the fact is, that definition in one's life is critical. If you don't know what you want and where you want to be, you're missing out on the opportunity that living in America affords. Also, you may be cheating yourself of living a happy, winning life in the undeniably easiest place on this planet to get it—America.

To determine if you're taking advantage of all that America offers or to reveal if you need to make some serious adjustments to where you want to be, ask yourself this important question:

QUESTION 1

**If I knew then what I know now, would I basically be
where I am and would I be doing what I'm now doing?**

Now, of course, just because you're not precisely
where you want to be doesn't mean that you're not on a
winning path. Most people have to tweak, enhance, enrich, and strive in their lives to make (or keep) it better no
matter where they are. But the question is…"Are you basically where you want to be?" "Are you basically in a life position that you are happy and comfortable with?"

For example, I always wanted to have a family, but I
also wanted a career. I wanted to be able to travel exten-
sively and I wanted a home that I was contented in and
proud of. Of course, I also had moments where I wanted to
be like Jane Goodall, living in a tent (well, maybe not a
tent, maybe a Marriott Courtyard) and studying the animals in the Serengeti, but not full-time. No, for full-time,
though there are always ways to make it better, I basically
wanted what I now have.

Now, if when answering Question 1 the answer was
"No," don't be frustrated, upset, or disheartened. Aristotle
said, "Self-awareness is the first step in change." And, you
have three options: (1) accept what you now have and
change your attitude to make the very best of it; (2) adjust
what you now have to make it better and to get it closer to
what you want; or (3) opt to make the major changes that
will help you get on the path to fulfill your life ambitions.

The point is that, if you want to, you have the power to change your life. You have the power to change your fate. You have the power to enhance your chances for happiness and success. You have the power to reposition your chances to win!

Louis L'Amour, the famous writer of cowboy tales, once said, "Up to a point a man's life is shaped by environment, heredity, movements and changes in the world about him. But then there comes a time when it lies within our grasp to shape the clay of our life into the sort of thing we wish it to be. Only the weak blame parents, their race, their times, their lack of good fortune, or the quirks of fate. The fact is that [especially in America] everyone has it within his or her power to say, 'This is what I am today, but that is what I might be tomorrow.' So begin by leveling with yourself. By asking and answering that first question, "Is this basically where I want to be?"

Now, if you're not where you want to be, you must do as most winners have done and move on to Question 2. Question 2 involves defining what it is that you want or where it is that you want to be. To get that answer, ask yourself this question:

QUESTION 2
What would I be doing now if I knew I couldn't fail at it?

At this point, don't think about what it would require to get you where you want to be. Don't think about the resources you might need to get there. Don't think about the things you'll have to deal with to get to there. Simply define where it is that you want to be or what it is that you want to do.

Many people spend a great deal of their precious time being bitter. They complain, moan, and groan about their lives. They never take the time to define what it would take to make them feel better; nor do they ever make the commitment to work out how to most happily live with what they currently have. Whether you change or stay where you are doesn't matter. That in itself has no bearing on winning. What you need to know is that to best position yourself to be a life winner, you need a sense of direction and a mindset that accepts that direction.

Now there is another question that must be asked, but this one is a tough one. It's, in fact, the rub. It's the comeback to reality from the dreaming question:

QUESTION 3
To get to where I want to be, can I live with the life changes I would need to make and be at peace in the pursuit process?

For example, once my children were born, I felt that I needed more creative outlets, and got involved in local theater. The thought of being a professional actress really appealed to me. However, I knew that to take that direction in my life would require giving up time and involvement with my family. Therefore, even if I took that direction and became a successful actress, I still wouldn't have been a winner, because taking my family out of my life would have cost me an important sense of internal peace and happiness.

There can be no doubt that you'll have to take a new, different, or more assertive course to get what you want. Changes in your life will have to be made. How much of a change is required? Is what you want worth giving up, or changing, what you now have? Is there a way to mitigate or control what you would have to give up? Is there a way to compromise that makes sense and feels good?

And now…the final question:

QUESTION 4
Am I willing to make the physical effort to do what it will take to get there?

Here, the question has to do with push, drive, will, and self-motivation. In other words, how hard are you personally willing to work for it? Keep in mind, that doing your best may not be enough. The question is, "Are you prepared to do what it will take?"

Now, if you're thinking, "Well, I can only do my best," you're wrong. You can push yourself harder. In fact, you can redefine your personal best. Often in life, to get where you want to go, to have what you want to have, you must stretch, reach, extend yourself more than you ever thought you could. I've been astounded by how much more people can achieve when necessity calls. I have also been astounded by how little people do when they can get away with it. If having to extend yourself is part of getting where you want to go, are you willing to do just that?

When I was a kid, I was taught to believe that if I would just do my best, that would be fine. After all, realistically, what else could there be? Doing one's best is all anyone could ever ask of anyone else. Doing my best was all I could ever ask of myself, right?

I recall coming home from middle school one year with a less than stellar report card. (I'm sure I didn't come right home.) In any event, since I arrived at dinnertime, both of my parents were seated at the kitchen table waiting for me. My father stretched out his hand for the report card. My mother (always the great anticipator) had her handkerchief poised near her eyes ready for the cry of defeat— "Where did we go wrong?"—and I wasn't going to disappoint her.

I reluctantly pulled that crumpled report card out of my jacket pocket and gave it to them. "Nicki, Nicki, Nicki," my father said, "How could you get a D in math? This isn't trigonometry or calculus—this is basic algebra. How could you get a D? I'm a CPA for heaven's sakes."

I remember crunching up my face and trying to look as sad and sincere as I possibly could. (George Burns once said that if you can fake sincerity, you've got it made). Then with a voice that was intended to show remorse, I answered, "I don't know how this happened. I tried. I tried. I really did. Math must not be my subject— because I tried my best."

"Did you? Did you try your best?" my parents asked in unison. "I did. I did," I reiterated. "Well," said my folks, "we're certainly not happy with this grade, but if you really did try your best, I guess that's all we can ask for."

Whew! "Is it really that easy?" I thought, "Hell, doing my best is okay." In fact, I bet that I can probably get away with anything if I just add the tag line "I did my best."

Well, folks, I might have been crazy, but I wasn't stupid, and I milked that phrase for everything it was worth. "I did my best" became my mantra. I had a handle. I liked it. I could relax. I could now explain any performance or effort that did not quite make it. I could do poorly and it would be acceptable. Mediocrity, here I come!

Well, I carried that phrase with me a long time. Oh yes, it helped me defend doing badly or at best being average. In fact, I could even capitalize on that phrase. I could purposely avoid working harder to do better—even when I could excel. People accepted it when I said I did my best… they had to.

Then I entered the real world—not the world of school, where learning is a passive experience (*they* supposedly teach *you*), but the world of business. Here I was trying to cope with the pressure of goals, demands, deadlines, expectations, and salary. What a nightmare.

I was, however, a quicker study than I thought. I soon learned that in reality we're not all equal. No, some of us set our limbo rod much lower than others. Some people seem to be able to actually better their best effort, or enhance their performance, when needed. Wait a minute here, isn't your best…your best?

The fact is that just as you can raise or lower your self-expectations; you can raise or lower your personal-best bar. You can do what you want to do and be where you want to be, if you are willing to redefine your best and reach higher.

Yes, you can most likely have it all if you are willing to dig a little deeper, work a little harder, expect a little more of yourself, and be ready and willing to do what it takes. So, the message is clear and simple: To get what you want may require doing more than your best. Are you ready to better your best? Are you ready to do what it takes?

When I think about the concept of doing what it takes, I'm reminded of what happens in California in March of every year. Yes, on March 19 of every year, the swallows return to San Juan Capistrano. Like clockwork every March, thousands upon thousands of little birds descend on this little town in Orange County to nest. And they come a long way. They come from Buenos Aires, Argentina. In other words, these little swallows fly about 6,000 miles to get to their nesting ground, and that's one hell of a trip without Dramamine. What makes that trip even more rigorous is that the majority of it is over water…and what makes it especially amazing is that swallows can't swim.

Well then, how do they make this journey? Do they actually keep flapping those little wings for 6,000 miles non-stop? Of course not, those wings would fall off. Instead, each swallow making this trip prepares for it before leaving Argentina. Each swallow before embarking on this remarkable journey picks up a twig off the ground with its beak. They hold that twig tightly as they fly over the ocean.

When it becomes necessary for them to take a rest, they quite simply drop the twig in the water and then float on it.

Once rested, they pick that twig up again in their beak, and carry it with them as they resume their journey to their next resting point. They do this maneuver over and over again until they arrive in Southern California.

Now that twig is a heavy burden for that swallow to carry for that distance, but they manage to do it. They manage to do it because they know where they want to go, and they are willing to do what it takes to get them there.

You see, if you want it badly enough, you can make it happen. It may not be easy, it may be a tough road, but if you're willing to pay the price, if you're willing to do what it takes, it can be yours.

So be a winner. Either get going on the journey that will take you where you want to go, or start finding peace and enjoyment with your current path. Life is too short to live with day-to-day dissatisfaction; either make it better or find a way to get happy with what you've got.

Chapter

15

Winning Principle

*Winners Know That Life Is Unfair
and the Hustle Never Really Ends*

For some, it may take a lifetime to realize that life is not fair. For others, they may never learn it. Winners, however, seem to understand that message early on in life and work within that context. No, life is not fair. I recall losing out on the opportunity to be interviewed by Tom Brokaw because I was flying at 35,000 feet when his office was trying to reach me for an impromptu interview—that's not fair! I remember losing out on the chance to work for the Department of Defense in Germany because my proposal simply got lost in the mail—that's not fair. I remember losing the prospect of perhaps being Sally, the girl who sobbed for her missing Saab automobile, when I misplaced the directions to the particular radio studio where the commercial was being cut. That's not fair. I remember losing four pounds (found those, and two more)—no, life is not fair. If life was fair, Elvis would still be alive and all those stupid impersonators would be dead.

Life is not fair, and it seems to be getting even more unfair. At one time, you could reach a certain modicum of business success and ride with that for a while. You could build a reputation for yourself, and while not resting perhaps on your laurels, you could at least exhale and coast on them for a while. Today, you are only as good as what you are doing right now! In today's world, you can't build a reputation based on future intentions and you can't keep a reputation based on past performance. There's a reason why Taco Bell, Coca-Cola, McDonalds, and all the other corporate giants spend multimillions every year to advertise. They keep hustling, don't they? Yet, the hustle is not a new concept. A top advertising executive told me that in 1987, General Foods spent 32 million dollars just to advertise Jell-O.

Ken Blanchard said that this is the first time in the history of business that you can be great at what you do today and be out of a job tomorrow. Life is not fair. We have all heard stories of people who were handed pink slips after 25 years of productive and loyal service to a company. We have all heard stories of people on the job who were replaced by someone with far less experience but who could be hired at a lower salary.

A similar experience happened to a friend of mine who worked for a large chemical company. Upon learning that he was being removed under the guise of early retirement, he was livid. He went to his superior stating that he was not ready to retire, cited the benefits he brought to the company, and talked about the value of his experience. His boss responded that experience is not what it used to be because change is happening so fast. Then he went on to elaborate that the company's decision was based on sound business logic. He explained that the company could continue to employ him as a researcher and pay him $75,000 a year—or, thanks to technology, telecommunications and computers—they can now work with a Russian Nobel Prize-winning researcher and pay him $175 dollars a month.

Winners always keep hustling. They accept the fact that the hustle doesn't end and they don't wallow or flounder in the unfairness of it all. Winners know that the minute they stop tap dancing, someone's going to steal their darn shoes. Winners know that when times are tough, they need the hustle to work *through* those tough times; they also know that when times are good, they need to hustle to take *advantage* of those good times.

My friend Ron from Phoenix loves cars. We're talking passion here. It's been said that cars are a guy thing. The comedienne Rita Rudner said that when someone asks her what kind of car she drives, she answers "white." Supposedly, men love cars and women love clothes. Now, it's stupid to generalize, however, I know that the only reason I like cars is that they get me to my clothes.

In any event, Ron recently purchased an old Jaguar to add to his collection, and he invested quite a bit of money in it. Some days it starts up, some days it doesn't. Ron's mechanic in Phoenix is Tony, originally from the Bronx. Tony loves cars too and is very, very macho. In fact, even Ron calls him Tony Testosteronie.

Ron was driving around in his Celica one afternoon and stopped in to see Tony to explain his dilemma with the Jag. "Hey, Tony," Ron said, "I need some advice about my old Jag. Sometimes it starts right up, and other times it won't budge. Should I bring it in? What should I do?" Tony thought for a minute, looked at Ron, and said, "Yeah, I got some advice for you. Next time it starts up, sell it!"

Though it may seem unfair that we must always be on the lookout to strike when the iron is hot, winners know how important that really is. Winners know that they can never quit hustling and that they have to keep hustling in both the good and the bad times.

Many people think that winners are just plain lucky. Many think that winners are those who happen to be in the right place at the right time. Many think that winners were fortunate enough to simply have the roulette wheel stop at their number. In reality, 99 percent of all winners make it happen, and they do that by honing those two critical hustling characteristics: **Discipline and Persistence.**

Discipline means doing what you should, when you should, whether you really want to do it or not. Discipline is indeed the basis of all greatness and is the foundation of winning. No matter what the general consensus of opinion may be— let me make this clear—all winners exhibit some form of discipline in their life.

Succinctly put, winners are quite simply the people who keep doing certain things that losers just don't want to do. Winners have a dedication to their plans, their dreams, and their goals. That dedication can turn into an obsession (and in that way, create a winner too), but it doesn't have to go to that extreme to move you into that winner's circle. You can win by having a more balanced approach than obsession; you can have that amazing, powerful blend of discipline mixed with persistence. To me discipline is the inner manifestation of control, but persistence is the outward manifestation of passion.

Many, many years ago, before it became fashionable, I joined a gym with my friend Barbara. We had great plans; we were going to work out every Monday, Wednesday, and

Friday night. We agreed that having to attend a business meeting was the only excuse we could use for missing a session. If we missed one of those prearranged weeknight exercise sessions because of work, we planned to make it up on the following Saturday morning.

Well, you know the story. We both started out like gangbusters. After the third week of this (and seeing no miraculous change in my body, I might add) I started looking for excuses. I began encouraging my clients to hold their meeting in the evenings, after work, so as not to interfere with the day's agenda. I started calling my own meetings at 6:00 P.M. You know the saying, "If you want to find a way, you will, and if you don't, you'll find an excuse." I found the excuse, lots of them in fact.

Barbara, however, continued on alone. She never called herself a disciplined person, but when it came to that gym, she went, whether she felt like it or not. We both needed the gym. But unfortunately in life it is not, "need and ye shall reap"; it is "plant and ye shall reap"—and planting takes discipline! Barbara planted herself on that treadmill three days a week for six months and won the body battle.

It doesn't matter whether you're trying to write a novel, become a gourmet cook, earn a degree in school, work out, or advance to the position of CEO. Discipline is a part of winning. Discipline means exercising control over yourself. Those who claim it was never part of their winning agenda are the obsessive types who become so immersed in their goals that their entire venture actually becomes one big discipline, to the exclusion of most other activities or interests.

Yes, while discipline is an inward control, persistence refers more to the outward actions we take. And remember, winners have both persistence and discipline.

Persistence counts! It has been said that nothing one can do can take the place of persistence. All the talent or ability in the world will not necessarily make it happen. There are thousands of able and talented people who are simply losers. Brilliance will not necessarily make winning happen either. The term unrewarded genius has become a platitude. Education alone won't make you a shoe-in. Educated failures are flipping burgers at McDonalds every day and filling out employment applications at Old Navy and The Gap.

I know a Princeton graduate who, with all her smarts, has never been able to keep a job. In fact, she's been out of work so long she now thinks W-2 refers to a Bingo number. After thirty years of studying winners, I've found that persistence is the one trait that is most positively correlated with winning.

Persistence involves a long-term perspective. Winners are those who, when working towards their objective or goal, refuse to quit when success is not easily seen on the horizon. They are the people who eventually seem to achieve the almost impossible. Of course, being persistent takes effort, stamina, and fortitude, so you have to be wise in selecting what you plan to become persistent about.

I'm reminded of the joke about the duck that went into a convenience store. The duck approached the clerk and asked, "Do you sell grapes here?" The clerk answered, "No, we don't." The next day, the same duck went back to the same convenience store, approached the same clerk, and asked, "Do you sell grapes here?" Again the clerk responded, "No, we don't!" The next day, the duck entered the same convenience store, went up to the same clerk, and asked, " Do you sell grapes here?" "What's wrong with you?" asked the clerk. "I told you, we don't sell grapes here." On day four, the duck entered the same convenience store, approached the same clerk, and asked, "Do you sell grapes here?" The clerk was livid. "I'm sick and tired of you coming in here asking for grapes. We don't sell grapes, and, if you come in here one more time asking for grapes, I'm going to nail your damn beak shut." The next day, the duck entered the convenience store, went up to the same clerk, and asked, " Excuse me, do you sell nails here?" The clerk responded, "No, we don't." "Okay," said the duck. "Then do you sell grapes?"

Yes, winners are persistent, but they pick and chose carefully what they will be persistent about. Persistence, by the way, as a trait, knows no age boundaries, as most parents of young children can well attest to.

Just recently, my two-and-a-half-year-old granddaughter, Zoe, was visiting. First we went shopping and then we returned back to my home at about 4:15 in the afternoon. Zoe joined me in the kitchen as I was figuring out dinner. With her big (and, I might unbiasedly add, beautiful) eyes, she looked up at me and asked, "Grandma, can I have some ice cream?" Considering the time of day, I answered, "No." Do you think she walked away and accepted my answer? Of course not. She stood right there and kept at me. I stood firm for a while. However, she finally wore me down. She simply refused to accept anything but what she wanted. Hopefully, this trait of tenacity and determination will remain with her in pursuing her positive goals in life.

Winners are the people who stay with it. Winners are committed to both discipline and persistence. Winners know the difference between making a decision and making a commitment. Remember, a decision is easy to make. We all make lots of decisions, every day. Decisions are logical; they are intellectual; they come from our head. However a commitment is another story. A commitment is hard to make because it's emotional; it comes from our heart. How many times do we hear about men or women in relationships who have decided to marry, but who still worry about the other's commitment to the relationship?

Yes, the hustle requires a commitment to discipline and persistence. It may be unfair that it never ends, but that's a fact of a winning life. You can't sustain a winning position without discipline and persistence.

So, start today to:

1. Immediately, select two positive actions that you can routinely take to enhance your work or home life. Remember, it was mentioned earlier that personal improvement leads to professional improvement; there-

fore it's perfectly acceptable to start with simple changes you can make and disciplines you can engage in even on the home front. It could be as simple as:

- Reading a chapter of a self-help book everyday.
- Drafting that to-do list each night in preparation for the next day.
- Laying out your clothes for work the night before.
- Making one extra follow-up call every work day.
- Organizing your desk before you leave the office for the day.
- Visiting a new business related website every evening.
- Connecting with a supplier or business partner to learn about what's new on their horizon each week.
- Cleaning out the refrigerator every weekend before you go shopping.
- Listening to a new language tape for 20 minutes twice a week.

2. Make the mental commitment to discipline yourself and persist with these two new actions so they turn into habits.

3. Every two weeks, add another positive discipline to your personal or professional repertoire.

4. Always leave some unstructured time in your agenda for spontaneity and flexibility. This will enable you to take advantage of opportunities that come along. Too much structure can lead to tunnel vision and lost chances.

5. Remember, it takes approximately 30 days for a new habit to set in and 90 days to break an old habit.

Your habits are critical in determining your winning opportunities in life. Habits will sustain you. In fact, habits are even more dependable than inspiration to spur you on to greatness or drag you down to defeat.

Discipline and persistence create habits. Discipline is about harnessing the mind-set and exercising the self-control necessary to turn a thought process or an action into habit. It involves creating a behavioral routine or establishing a personal regimen. Discipline is mechanical in nature.

Persistence is about having the burn, the desire, the motivation, and the passion to relentlessly pursue, to keep at it, to prevail. Persistence is more emotional in nature.

The power of positive discipline and persistence working together will tip the scales in your favor in an unfair world. In fact, discipline and persistence define the term "hustle" in the more positive light it deserves.

Winning Principle

*Winners Understand
the Real Rules of Life*

Rules—the hell with them. When we were kids, we had to obey them. As we got older, it seemed that so many of them just beckoned to be broken. As mature adults, we understand that though civilizations need rules to function, so many rules that were at one time relevant regarding our personal as well as our business lives just don't apply anymore. On the other hand, it seems that perhaps some rules of the past that have gone by the wayside need to be revived. In this age of moral relativism, it seems that determining rules to live by is confusing at best.

I was talking to one of my clients in Florida about the inapplicability of many old business rules. We were trying to out-do each other by coming up with one irrelevant rule after another. However, I think she topped me when she said that there is a Florida rule that requires exotic dancers to have at least one-third of their rear ends covered while working. What an inapplicable rule. We agreed that it was stupid to have that rule for exotic dancers; that rule should be made for plumbers.

Now don't get me wrong. It's not that some of the old rules don't matter anymore. It's just that most of us have learned that for the most part all does not come to those who wait, it's not just as easy to marry a rich man as it is a poor one, and that the good do not get rewarded and the bad do not get punished (at least not in this lifetime).

Crosby, Stills, and Nash sing a song about ethics, morals, and the rules of life. "You, who are on the road, must have a code, that you can live by." Winners know how true this is.

Winners do indeed seem to have a code of rules they live and work by. They know, selecting from the bevy of rules they grew up with, what rules stay and what rules go. They know what rules apply today and what rules don't; and no matter what others seem to do, they march on with their code.

Here are some of those crucial rules that winners embrace. Some have proven their applicability, worthiness, and staying power over the years. Others may be somewhat new to you. Adherence to these rules constitutes an important role in positioning yourself to win—and remember positioning yourself to win is even more important than wanting to win. So, take an important step, review and maybe even revamp the codes of life you live by. See if your rules match up with the common rules winners win by. Where do you stand?

1. *Good thoughts lead the way to a good life.* Yes, if you want a better life, think better thoughts. Our lives do indeed tend to gravitate toward our dominant thoughts. Remember the drag-to-lift ratio. That simple aeronautical principle states that a plane can't take off if its drag exceeds its lift. Well, the same concept applies to you. You can't take off if your drag exceeds your lift. Negative thoughts serve as your most significant drag. Winners do what it takes to eliminate those negative thoughts from their mind. Do you?

   Check: _____ Or: _____
             Yes   No

2. *Your life improves when you improve.* Winners know that if you want a different or better life you must understand that you will have to do different or better things. Winners understand that if you keep on doing what you always did, you set yourself up to keep on getting what you always got. Now, if what you have is exactly what you want, keep on doing what you're now doing. However, if it isn't, are you ready to make changes?

   Check: _____ Or: _____
         Yes   No

3. *Ninety percent of winning starts with a positive attitude.* Though, as we learned in previous chapters, a positive attitude is just the beginning, it is indeed a powerful and essential beginning. Having a positive attitude is not a hit-and-miss feeling; it is an everyday choice that you have control over. Every single day you have a choice as to what attitude you will embrace and project for that day. Are you choosing to have a good attitude on a day-to-day basis?

   Check: _____ Or: _____
         Yes   No

4. *Happiness in life is not based upon what's dealt you; it is based upon how you react and how you respond to what's dealt you.* I know several people who seem to have excellent luck. On paper they have it all. You could say that the roulette wheel of life has favored

them. Yet, they are not happy people by any stretch of the imagination.

On the other hand, I know many people who have had to deal with misfortune and hardships beyond their control who are very happy people. Think about this rule: Happiness is part of that winning definition and it is not a future event or circumstance; it is an everyday outlook. Life is like a game of cards. You have no control over the hand that is dealt you, but you have total control over how that hand is played out. Do you try to react and respond positively to life? Do you avoid being swept up by feeling victimized?

Check: _____ Or: _____
          Yes   No

5. *Act and live your life as if no one is coming to your rescue.* I adore Aretha Franklin when she belts out "Rescue Me," but winners understand that the old rule "If it is to be, it is up to me" still applies. Winners put themselves in charge of themselves. Do you accept responsibility for yourself?

Check: _____ Or: _____
          Yes   No

6. *What got you where you are is not going to be enough to keep you there.* Though I mentioned this fact earlier on, it is critical to understand that today products and people have, for the most part, a shorter shelf life than

ever before in history. We must always be growing, learning, and bettering ourselves. Einstein said, "The significant problems we face cannot be solved at the same level of thinking we were at when they were created." Your worth to your company is based on how good you are at what you are doing now, right now. Therefore, you must keep learning so that you can be exposed to the newest concepts and techniques that can help you do what you do in an outstanding way.

Remember, new concepts enhance your ability to think and new techniques enhance your ability to perform. For the true professional, the learning seminar is never over. You must know what you are doing so well that you get known by others for what you are doing. Yes, the challenge today is not just getting that education; it's keeping it. Forty percent of people pursuing degrees today are over 40, so join the movement. Are you currently in the process of learning something new?

Check: _____ Or: _____
       Yes   No

7. *Make yourself essential to your customer.* Your job security today will be, in most instances, based on how valuable you are the customer. Though no one is indispensable, you must still make every effort to make yourself needed, wanted, and necessary. Do you approach *your* job in such a way that your customers go

out of *their* way to make certain that your company knows how special and important a person you are?

Check: _____ Or: _____
      Yes   No

8. *Birds of a feather do indeed tend to flock together.* Winners know they need to watch their choice of friends and associates. Since we, as human beings, seem to be greatly influenced by others in our circle, it's wise to ask yourself these questions from time to time:

   - Who am I spending time with?
   - Where do they have me going?
   - How do they have me looking?
   - What do they have me saying?
   - What do they have me seeing?
   - What do they have me reading?
   - How do they have me thinking?
   - What do they have me accepting?
   - What do they have me planning?
   - What do they have me becoming?

   Then, of course, the message is loud and clear. If your field of influence is not helping you to become the kind of person you wish to become, you must change the field. Winners know that negative people have an almost mysterious ability to sell—and pass on—their negativity. Winners know that if they must, due to family responsibilities (or the like) be around negative people, they do all in their power to minimize the time spent with them.

About four times a year we visit an aunt who starts off every conversation with, "Guess who died?" We vowed, next year, dinner would only be twice! Are you spending time with people who are good for you, your attitude, and your life goals?

Check: _____ Or: _____
　　　　Yes　　　　　　　No

9. *Luck favors the prepared.* Stay ready, willing, and able to seize opportunities. Those who say they never had an opportunity are usually the ones who never seized an opportunity. They are the people who find excuses why the timing was not right. To seize opportunities, you must stay alert. Winners stay ready for opportunities that can improve, enhance, or better their lives. I love to travel, and I'm always ready to go. If someone calls and invites me on an impromptu trip, I can literally be ready in one hour flat. Do you plan ahead to be able to take advantage of potential opportunities?

Check: _____ Or: _____
　　　　Yes　　　　　　　No

10. *You are what you do.* Positive thoughts are the prerequisite, but positive action is the only thing that makes anything happen. Winners know that at times they have to push themselves to take action. They know that most of the time the greatest things in life happen when you make yourself do something that you were too tired, too

preoccupied, or too scattered to do. Most of the useful work in this world is done by people who are crunched for time, tired, or not feeling especially well.

Winners also know that action is more than just doing. It's making something happen as a result of the effort. Winners never confuse movement with action. Rather than succumb to laziness, are you an action-oriented person?

Check: _____ Or: _____
         Yes   No

11. *Take care of your number-one asset—you.* The only way you'll be able to make the most of yourself is to take care of yourself. It's not narcissistic to give yourself some personal attention. Do what winners do:

- With doctor's approval, exercise and work up a sweat for 30 minutes three times a week. Personally, I have found that the best time for me to exercise is in the morning before my brain figures out what the heck I'm doing!

- Practice relaxation techniques. Massage therapists are a great source to learn how to do this. Yoga classes can work magic as well.

- Limit caffeine and eat well. Though in today's world it seems that the four basic food groups have become fast, frozen, carryout, and delivered, the old rule, you are what you eat, still has credence. So how many of you are fast, cold, cheap, and easy? Get a full-length mirror and look at your body. Realize you're not renting that body; you've bought it. That's your home. This is where you live. Treat it well.

- Balance your life. Sleep, rest, downtime, and fun are part of the productive and regenerative keys to life. The cemeteries out there are filled with indispensable people. Balance is critical to a winning life. Do you have it in yours? Are you taking care of you?

Check: _____ Or: _____
      Yes   No

12. *Work hard.* Even though you may have talent, you must still work hard. When considering talent and hard work, remember hard work still takes the prize if talent won't work hard. Do you consider yourself a hard worker? Are you willing to put the effort in?

Check: _____ Or: _____
      Yes   No

13. *Tell the truth.* By telling the truth, you will have so much less to remember. At the very least, keeping track of lies can overwhelm and exhaust you. Are you a truthful person?

Check: _____ Or: _____
      Yes   No

14. *Be adaptable when necessary.* Choose your battles well. Every year for a week or so my husband and I go sailing with some of our friends. My friend and captain, Kim Muller, taught me that there is a rule in sailing that

states that the more maneuverable ship should yield to the less maneuverable one. Often you will find that this rule can work to your advantage in relationships with others as well as on the high seas. Though winners do not give up what they stand for, they don't make a cause out of every little thing. They pick and choose wisely. They know when to stand firm and when to give in. They understand that if a situation comes to pass where they need to be adaptable in order to move forward, they're not afraid to bend when called for. Can you be adaptable when necessary?

Check: _____ Or: _____
       Yes   No

15. *Stop complaining.* Winners don't complain; instead they either try to fix it or move on with it. Maya Angelou said, "If you don't like something change it; if you can't change it, change your attitude about it. But stop complaining." Do you find yourself to be a chronic complainer or can you express yourself and move on without grumbling?

Check: _____ Or: _____
       Yes   No

16. *Give up what you want now for what you want most.* Winners can avoid making the easier choice, just because it is easier. Winners know that if a decision has to be made, they often have to control the temptation to choose the easier solution. They're aware that what often seems easier at the moment will result in much

more work later on. Winners are willing to give up what they want now for what they want most. That is true vision. Are you willing to give up what you want now for what you want most?

Check: _____ Or: _____
          Yes   No

17. *Winners understand what constitutes self-esteem and practice to keep theirs high.* Winners know that self-esteem has nothing to do with formal education, innate intelligence, looks, net worth, family background, breeding, or even success. Having self-esteem means more than having self-confidence; it entails having a sense of self-worth. Self-esteem is what you think of yourself—and that's a much more important element in winning than what others think of you. In fact self-improvement won't matter much if you don't have self-esteem first. However, to reiterate, don't confuse self-esteem with a feeling of self-importance. Self-importance intimates that you feel you are more significant than others, and that's not at all what real self-esteem is about.

Yes, self-esteem is about having a sense of self-value and self-acceptance. So many people have the wrong idea as to how to get self-esteem; yet the condition of your self-esteem is critical, as it defines and portrays your life at any given time.

By having self-esteem, you bring to yourself amazing power as well as resilience. Your self-esteem affects your general health, your vitality, your goal setting and goal getting, your peace and contentment, your relationships with others, your abilities, and your performance.

There are six major elements that contsitute a sense of self-esteem. Check to make certain these elements are in your life.

- *Self-reliance:* It is very difficult to have self-esteem if you don't feel that you can take care of yourself. Having self-reliance doesn't mean that you will not or cannot accept help, advice, guidance, gifts, property, or even cash from others. Instead, it implies that if need be, you can do for yourself. If need be, you can do what it takes to earn a living, take care of yourself, and take care of the children you are responsible for. Remember, act as if no one is coming to your rescue.

- *Self-achievement:* Self-esteem requires that you feel a personal sense of achievement in your life. Understand, however, that the achievement we are talking about here does not have to be monumental or unique; it just has to involve something that you accomplished in which you feel a sense of pride. Whether it's the achievement of being an involved and interested parent, a fine bridge player, an excellent book-keeper, an articulate speaker, a creative cook, an outstanding hostess, a recognized authority, or one of the fastest hackers, feeling that you have achieved something in your life is essential to gaining that sense of self-esteem.

- *Self-control:* When people take control of themselves, big changes occur that go far beyond the obvious. A colleague, after years of trying, finally stopped smoking. He called to tell me how great he felt about conquering his smoking habit and how much better he felt about himself in general. His good feelings came about from his power to exercise self-control. So it was more than food that tasted better once he stopped puffing: It was a sense of being in charge that was so magnificent and empowering.

Therefore, whether it's controlling the impulse to skip the treadmill today, controlling your ability to keep you caloric intake down, or controlling your need to always play devil's advocate, bringing self-control into your life will bring you closer to having self-esteem.

- *Self- expression:* There's a definite correlation between those who are able to express themselves and those who have self-esteem. Therefore, if you have someone in your life who you can talk to frankly, who will listen, and who will not pass judgment, consider yourself a person who has the gift of self-expression. However, self-expression can be gained in other ways as well. Perhaps you paint or draw; maybe you keep a journal or write short stories; maybe you dance or are musically inclined. All those activities allow you to express yourself as well. Therefore, though self-expression can take many forms, you have to have an expression outlet in your life to have a sense of self-esteem.

- *Self-praise:* In this book, I mentioned the importance of using affirmations to help you better motivate yourself, and I highlighted the significance of saying nice things when you talk to yourself. However, the key is to make this a habit. Yes, pat yourself on the back whenever you can.

To some, using affirmation cards may seem hokey. To those who use them, they can be miraculous. Simply by saying certain phrases to yourself repeatedly, with feeling and determination, you will note a real change in your self-perception. I recommend either collecting phrases you like the sound of or writing your own phrases down on index cards, one phrase per card. Put an elastic band around them and take them with you wherever you go. Commit to reading them to yourself at least four times a day— in the morning, afternoon, evening, and right before you go to bed. The key is to stick to it, without fail, for one full month. Winners know how taking this step can make a vital change in one's self-perception and serve to contribute to a positive, often dramatic change in your life.

Here the "fake it before you make it" syndrome comes again into play. So when you read those affirmations, do so with earnestness, and sound convincing. The more vitality, believability, and feeling you put into saying your affirmations, the quicker they will work toward helping you to naturally praise yourself and feel the benefit of this exercise. Phrases such as:

"I will make a sale this week."
"I am in the process of achieving my goals."
"I am a person of value."
"I am not afraid to take a chance."
"I have faith in myself."
" I focus in on the positives."
"I have the power to make what I want, happen."
"I am a person who will fight for what I want and get it."
"I deserve to have my dreams come true and they will."

So whether the task is self-motivation or worthiness, winners know how important it is to include these self-affirmations in their life, especially if they find their self-esteem temporarily lagging.

- *Self-giving:* If you're ever in doubt as to your self-worth, do yourself and others a big favor. Give your time and attention to anyone who is less fortunate than you. For example, volunteer to help out at the local hospital one weekend morning, visit a nursing home and just sit there and talk to a resident for 30 minutes or so every week, serve food at the homeless center on a routine basis, and so on. It's amazing how these simple acts of kindness will affect your perception of yourself. You will truly see how valuable you are just by giving of yourself to those who are in need of comfort, help, caring, attention, or food. Taking this step is one of the quickest ways to help you recognize your self-worth.

Remember, if you feel unworthy of respect, success, and happiness, no one else will feel you are worthy either. Self-esteem is the first step before peer esteem. Do you consciously make an effort to keep your self-esteem high?

Check: _____ Or: _____
       Yes   No

18. *Count your blessings each and every day.* Make thankfulness a daily habit. This simple act will help you keep things in perspective. Do you take the time to be thankful every day for what you have?

Check: _____ Or: _____
       Yes   No

Walt Disney believed that if you can dream it, you can do it. Many people forget the "do it" part. Life is indeed a great and magnificent mystery. However, all we really know for certain is what we have right here, right now, at this very moment. Winners plan for tomorrow but they know how to make the very best out of today. Recognize that since you live in a free country, it is indeed up to you. You can reach for the moon, and you can get there. Open your eyes, do what winners do, see what winners see, and take advantage of all you've got going for you. We live in a time of great opportunities. Don't miss it.